"Oh my. WHAT A BOOK! This is the book ⟨...⟩ raro answers the question many of us have: W⟨...⟩ changer in the self-development field, and I can't ⟨...⟩

—**Dr. Peta Stapleton**, associate professor of psychology
and author of *The Science Behind Tapping*

"Kris Ferraro takes the shame out of being (feeling different) and turns it into a superpower strength. Her book is a brilliant collection of healing tools and transformative exercises." —**Sherianna Boyle**, author of *Emotional Detox Now*

"Welcome to the new normal, where being weird and different are superpowers. This heartwarming, personable account of her journey is inspiring and challenging in the perfect ways and generously full of supportive resources. A must-read for pioneers, visionaries, and all desiring to feel and be more themselves everywhere."
—**Sydney Campos**, bestselling author, visionary, and transformational healer

"If you were told . . . 'just be yourself,' and you find yourself looking for a guide who's been there and done that, someone who will help you not just through example, but with practices that you can make your own, . . . [this] is the book for you. [Kris] is a fiercely loving and relatable role model and teacher. This book is a joyful, full-body YES!"

—**Karen C. L. Anderson**, M2T, master-certified life
coach, and author of *You Are Not Your Mother*

"[Y]ou'll find camaraderie and courage on every page. Liberating, funny, and practical, the tales and experiential exercises offer a flexible and fun road map. All aboard to find an embrace of your difference that brings an abiding sense of wholeness, in safe, loving company."

—**Jondi Whitis**, master trainer for EFT International and
author of *Emotional First-Aid for Children*

"Kris Ferraro points the way to a freer destination. While many books promise this by offering a compass that points reliably north, Ferraro gifts the rest of us a compass where the needle dances erratically, defying the conventional pull of normal, leading to uncharted territory and unexplored paths. . . . *Your Difference Is Your Strength* offers a magnificent, scenic, authentic road home."

—**Catherine A. Duca**, LCSW, psychotherapist, speaker, trainer and author of *Unmasked*

"ALL HAIL THE QUEEN OF THE MISFITS! . . . *Your Difference Is Your Strength* is the much-needed manifesto for anyone who has ever felt like an outsider. . . . If you have been holding yourself back in any area of life because you don't fit in, this book will remind you how much of a treasure you are!"

—**Ilona Pamplona**, astrology-informed life coach and author of *This Journal Is Your Mood Ring*

"This book has the wisdom of a self-help book but the exciting, quick read of a novel. The takeaway: You are not alone. Lean into your unique differences as your superpower and strength."

—**Robin Bilazarian**, LCSW, DCEP, researcher, psychotherapist, and author of *Tapping the Mighty Mind*

"This wonderful book offers a message of hope, empowerment, and self-acceptance along with tools and practices that are truly life-changing. . . . This book belongs in every library, high school guidance counselor's office, and college bookstore in the world."

—**Jennifer Elizabeth Moore**, author of *Empathic Mastery*, host of the *Empathic Mastery Show* podcast, and master trainer for EFT International

"Kris Ferraro is like a kind, sassy older sister who's been there and done that. She skillfully shares her wild stories, wise inspiration, and deep encouragement in this wonderful manifesto for all of us freaks. Dive in and learn to embrace your unique self."   —**Nikki Starcat Shields**, book midwife, writing retreat host, and author of *The Heart of the Goddess*

"This is a must-read for anyone who knows they move to beat of their own drummer but wants to share that beat with the world."

—**Gene Monterastelli**, editor at TappingQandA.com and host of the *Tapping Q&A Podcast*

"An anthem for those of us who feel like we're from the island of misfit toys. Kris Ferraro lovingly scripts the balm for every soul that's been bullied, left out, and left behind."   —**Britt Bolnick**, successful biz owner and bestselling author of *The Magick of Bending Time in Your Sacred Business*

"[A] valuable road map that will help anyone who has ever felt like they were 'different' in any way, process their pain, step into their innate power, and claim their unique gifts!"   —**Bonnie Durkin**, empowerment coach and author of *The Appreciation Game*

"*Your Difference Is Your Strength* is for all of us who have ever felt like the misfit or the outsider. This book is the friend we wished we'd had whose loving shines a light on all that makes us unique and turns our pain into our power."

—John O'Neill, Broadway music director

Your Difference Is Your Strength

A Guide to Accepting Yourself—for Anyone Who Has Ever Felt Out of Place

KRIS FERRARO

ST. MARTIN'S
ESSENTIALS
NEW YORK

First published in the United States by St. Martin's Essentials,
an imprint of St. Martin's Publishing Group

YOUR DIFFERENCE IS YOUR STRENGTH. Copyright © 2023 by Kris Ferraro. All rights reserved.
Printed in the United States of America. For information, address St. Martin's Publishing
Group, 120 Broadway, New York, NY 10271.

www.stmartins.com

The Library of Congress Cataloging-in-Publication Data is available upon request.

ISBN 978-1-250-87519-8 (trade paperback)

ISBN 978-1-250-87520-4 (ebook)

Our books may be purchased in bulk for promotional, educational,
or business use. Please contact your local bookseller or the Macmillan
Corporate and Premium Sales Department at 1-800-221-7945, extension 5442,
or by email at MacmillanSpecialMarkets@macmillan.com.

First Edition: 2023

10 9 8 7 6 5 4 3 2 1

For the last picked,
perpetually dismissed,
the overlooked, underseen,
and everyone in between.
Every word of this is for you.

Contents

Foreword

Maybe you've felt different from others and wished you could fit in. But what if you could not only accept yourself *exactly the way you are* but celebrate and amplify what makes you a singular powerhouse? You hold that ticket in your hands.

I wish I'd read this book years ago. It might have spared me a thousand journal pages and a wad of therapy bills. Like many of us, I fought my difference. I tried desperately to do the "right things," things others told me were rational and commendable, even when they made me feel like an impostor.

I wasn't an obvious misfit. Actually, I could "play normal" pretty well. I graduated from Harvard Law School and pleased my New York City Jewish parents and school guidance counselors everywhere. I got a high-paying job on the partnership track of a big law firm. But all the while, I felt like this undercover oddball. Something was missing for me—meaning, oxygen, and soul. Everyone said I had success. But I felt like I had a picture of success, and the real me wasn't in that picture.

It was only when I walked out of everything without a plan, got a job waiting tables, dated a long-haired tarot card reader, and started writing that I felt alive for the first time. Yep, I looked like a weirdo. I shocked my family. But I could breathe. I felt more alive than I'd ever felt in my life.

And when I finally honored this true spirit within me, I wrote the books I needed to write and started teaching and coaching others. I even became a national expert on career transformation. I have helped thousands or tens of thousands of others to discover and live their callings. And I'm just one person who listened to the difference inside herself. Can you imagine the impact on this planet if we all honored what made us different?

I think Kris Ferraro imagines this for us. And her bold, fun, brilliant book *Your Difference Is Your Strength* is the permission you may have needed to be the most audacious, wondrous version of yourself. The world doesn't give you guideposts for how to turn your differences into the tools of a trailblazer. But Kris Ferraro does. In this book, you will find the healing of being acknowledged, seen, and encouraged. You will find techniques that help you regain your power. She gives you movies to watch, soundtracks to listen to, and examples of other Misfits who transformed into Trailblazers—and contributed to the lives of others.

We live in a world that is changing. We are charged with embracing diversity because, as Kris Ferraro says, our difference is our strength. Think about the greatest innovations and movements in business, medicine, creativity, and politics. The best of what we are hasn't come from people who are trying to match the status quo. We move forward and sideways because of people who think and breathe and see things differently. It takes people who are different to help us to do things differently.

I shared this in my book *Inspired & Unstoppable*, and I will share it here: "As a creative, individual visionary leader, independent thinker, soul healer, or entrepreneur, it's your birthright to utilize other talents, insights, resources, and innate strategies. You are not made to fit into the world, make it *in* the world, but to remake the world, heal the world, and illuminate new choices and sensibilities. . . . Obey your rebel brilliance." We are living in times with new challenges. But our new solutions will come from misfits, those who are alternatively gifted and original.

Some of you may feel as though you're just trying to get by, never mind saving the world. Kris Ferraro is here to address you wherever you are and take you on a journey of bravery. You've got a great guide in Kris. She's so real. She's lovable. She's wise. And make no mistake, she is a force of nature. If you've ever hoped to have an ally, someone who really got you and stood up for you, you've found her. She takes every ounce of her personal pain and alchemizes it into perspective, wisdom, and moxie for us all.

Your Difference Is Your Strength needs to be shared. And this message needs to be sung from rooftops. I hope these words are read far and wide. And most of all, I hope that more of us begin to embody this message, because we are all misfits in some way. We have shied away from our big talents, instinctive leanings, or true voices at some point. And maybe this is the book that will help you to stand strong in your wobbling, awkward, dazzling, one-of-a-kind, gift-to-this-planet self. I hope you do. And I'm so grateful that Kris Ferraro has risen in her power to sound the call.

May we all find our own brilliant way.

—Tama Kieves

Tama Kieves is a *USA Today*–featured visionary career coach and is the bestselling author of *Thriving Through Uncertainty* and *A Year Without Fear*. Visit her at www.tamakieves.com.

Introduction

The Square Peg Abandons the Round Hole

"NO ONE IS YOU AND THAT IS YOUR GREATEST POWER."

—DAVE GROHL

I always just *knew*. There was never a before time. Never a simple moment of forgetting. Not ever a time when I just felt "normal." Whatever that is. As I grew through childhood into adolescence and later adulthood, there were the more obvious external signs. The unconventional body type. The commanding voice. All that wacky creativity. The mystical leanings where I talked to the Universe, animals, and trees. That time in eighth grade when I had my hair cut into a crew-cut with the tips of my naturally black hair dyed blond. My attraction to music and movements outside the mainstream.

Hi, let me introduce myself. I'm Kris, and I'm just *different*. I've gone by many labels. Ones others have placed on me and ones I've recognized within myself. Loser. Weirdo. Freak. Misfit. Rebel. Mystic. Empath. And while on the outside I don't look like a success story or an inspiration, the truth is that in the uncovering of who I truly am, I've become the star of my own sweet world. I'm here not only to take the road less traveled but also to blaze a brand-new path forward into original realms. And *that* is something no mainstream "winner" person could ever do. I was born with a spiritual and creative calling that was beckoning me to stop searching for and trying to become worthy of the acceptance of "them." My Higher Self knew that was never going to happen and that it could never provide what I longed for: to be understood, accepted, cherished, and loved.

As early as grade school, I immersed myself in biographies, reveling in true tales of those who won at the game of life. If I could figure out how they did it, then maybe I could do it. What I found shocked me. All those visionaries and creative geniuses? Every single one of them had an origin story similar to mine. They weren't born into prestige and unwavering support. No one looked at them and said, "You are destined to become someone!" Their peers didn't shower them with adoration. No, not at all. They started out as Misfits, just like me. They used their adversity and passion to become Trailblazers. Decades in, I knew. The Misfit and the Trailblazer are two sides of the same archetype, sharing the same sacred destiny to advance life forward.

I knew. "I'm not alone."

You'd have only picked this book up if you knew this too. You're just different, in ways both subtle and not.

Maybe you feel different because of:

- *the way you feel*
- *the way you look*
- *the way you act*
- *how your brain or body works*
- *who you are attracted to*
- *who your family is (or isn't)*
- *how much money you have (or don't have)*
- *your education*
- *your interests*

- *where you live*
- *or a million other things . . .*
- *or maybe all of the above*

In ways obvious or invisible, you were created as a unique being. You were born into a culture of conformity that doesn't always value uniqueness. You may not have been welcomed with acceptance. Instead, you've likely internalized a message that goes against your very nature: Me, I'm a problem. Defective. Off. Wrong. Bad. Weird. Shameful. Broken. Deformed. Unwanted. Impossible. Doomed. Cursed.

You may have been labeled by others: Loser. Freak. Misfit. Pariah. Outcast. Weirdo.

To me, you are Beloveds. I am so happy you are here.

You may not fully believe me yet (though you probably have an inkling), but inside of you a hero's journey is about to begin. You are exactly the way you are for a reason. You didn't come here to follow the status quo. You didn't come here to amble mindlessly along well-trodden territory. You're not here to be "acceptable." You were not created to follow the crowd. You're certainly not here to be like everyone else.

> ## "IF YOU ARE ALWAYS TRYING TO BE NORMAL, YOU WILL NEVER KNOW HOW AMAZING YOU CAN BE."
>
> —MAYA ANGELOU

You're here to be extraordinary. In your own unique way.

You may scoff or doubt. Underneath, there may be no small amount of quivering. I've expected that. Years ago, if anyone had pulled me aside and shared these sentiments, here's exactly how I would have reacted: "What the heck do you know?!"

This has been my journey too. To unchain myself from others' small ideas. To take the stick-figure versions of myself, interchangeable with a million others, and burn them to the ground.

I've been sent here from your future selves. Or your inner children. Or your precious, perfect souls, waiting to launch their sacred mission. I've been sent from the atrocities of the past. Or the revolutions of the present. Likely I've been sent from a vibrant future that needs you and your gifts to be created, explored, exposed, and shared.

There are gifts within you that have yet to emerge. You don't have a hint of their existences yet. They're going to ask of you what you may not think you're capable of delivering. And then there are the gifts you've been keeping hidden out of fear of being shamed.

You're always going to be different. No amount of external fixes can change that. Isn't it time to embrace your full self with all its quirks and hidden treasures?

It's time to *stop*.

Stop hiding.

Stop making yourself invisible.

Stop settling for less than you deserve.

Stop being treated like an enemy, a pariah, or an inconvenience.

Stop stifling your ideas, your artistry, and your unconventional brilliance.

Stop trying to be like others so you can fit in.

Stop accepting a destiny that is choking your true essence like a dark shroud.

In this book you are going to find my story, as well as the stories of many others who went from mere Misfit to triumphant Trailblazer. You'll also find questions to ask yourself at the end of each chapter, along with clarifying exercises. I recommend buying a journal so you can answer those questions and keep track of your feelings and thoughts along the way. Write down what you like, what you don't like, what you agree with, what you don't agree with, and every other thing you want to express. This is your safe space to say whatever you want without self-judgment and censorship. Maybe you can even put a big logo on the front that says M2T, which stands for "Misfit to Trailblazer." You don't even have to explain what it means to others; it can be our secret. When I have something that I want to suggest you write in the journal, we'll call it an M2T Journal Moment.

And speaking of M2T, once you start emerging out of your shell, feel free to turn it into a #hashtag. This will help all of us M2Ts to find one another, offer support, and celebrate the hardest thing we can ever do: be fully ourselves.

To support you in your journey, I've created a website with multimedia resources. At www .yourdifferenceisyourstrength.com you'll find PDFs of all the exercises, so you can print them out and make a notebook. There are also audio visualizations, affirmations, Spotify playlists, and more.

This book is my love letter to you.

And along with that, it's a call for a revolution! A revolution of radical self-love and self-acceptance. A revolution for inner freedom to be who our souls came here to be.

Join me!

> **"THE VAST MAJORITY OF HUMAN BEINGS DISLIKE AND ACTUALLY DREAD ALL NOTIONS WITH WHICH THEY ARE NOT FAMILIAR—HENCE IT COMES ABOUT THAT AT THEIR FIRST APPEARANCE INNOVATORS HAVE GENERALLY BEEN PERSECUTED, AND ALWAYS DERIDED AS FOOLS AND MADMEN."**
>
> —ALDOUS HUXLEY

M2T Journal Moment

1. *What makes you different? Start with the obvious and keep writing until the deeper truths emerge.*

2. *Write down a time when you were labeled, judged, and/or excluded.*

3. *Share negative things you say or think about yourself.*

MISFIT TO TRAILBLAZER (M2T) POWER TERMS

"Normality is a fine ideal for those who have no imagination."
— CARL JUNG

The power terms, used interchangeably, are:

Universe, Love, God, Spirit, and Higher Self.

What They Are: The energy that inhabits all. An invisible substance that is composed of creative ideas, creative process, and what is created, all in one. That which takes form as everything we can see and all that is invisible. Everything that has ever existed or will ever exist. The atoms and molecules at the center of all matter. The source of all. Everything we love and everything we don't. Oneness. All Love. All Life. Ever-expanding good. Interconnectivity. The power that created every element in the periodic table. That which creates hydrogen and oxygen and brings them together to compose water— including the water that makes up most of your body, and mine. Power. The force. The alpha and the omega. Yin and yang. Wholeness. Infinity.

What They Are Not: Condemning. Judging. Punishing. Isolating. Duality. Dogma. Separate from us. Approving of certain kinds of people and not approving of other kinds of people. Needing our obedience, approval, and belief. Suppression. An old man on a cloud, or any man, or a person of any other assigned gender[1] for that matter, waiting to strike you down if you don't follow the current rules according to others.

---

[1] Deities usually have a gender identity. You may indeed connect with this invisible force I'm calling the Universe via a deity that will likely have an ascribed gender. That's not only perfectly fine, but it can also make deepening this most important relationship easier. Deities have human-constructed images and ideas about what they look and sound like. This can make them an ideal focal point for you to turn to for support.

When I write the power terms, see and hear whatever name works for the higher power of your understanding.

Misfit: A person who isn't considered suitable, acceptable, adequate, or similar enough to receive the welcoming acceptance and inclusion of others, who have recognized this difference. A free, often out-of-the-box thinker.

Trailblazer: A person who illuminates or spearheads a new or alternative path to the one that, until now, has been accepted. An innovator, a pioneer, a groundbreaker, even a trendsetter. Someone who refuses to tamper with their true identity and their vision.

Misfit to Trailblazer (M2T): The journey from healing the pain of standing alone to embracing your unique essence to sharing unapologetically with the world.

Extraordinary Ordinaries: Average, normal, everyday moments in which you have an extraordinary, often mystical, inspirational, or creative, internal experience. You've asked for a sign, and you receive it. You're filled with awe at a scene you've come across.

Example: The character Sam Obisanya on the television show *Ted Lasso*. Sam, a rising Nigerian football (soccer) star for Richmond, considers leaving his team for an option to play for a future African league. His father encourages him to "ask the Universe." Sam sees a kid playing football in the grass and notices he's wearing a shirt with Sam's name and number on it. The scene turns to fuzzy slow motion to indicate he's having an Extraordinary Ordinary. He takes this as a sign to stay at Richmond.

Example: Standing in your shower when you get the most brilliant idea for a product you'd like to create. You're not at a four-star hotel. No, it's just your ordinary shower on an ordinary day. But something incredible is unfolding within you. It feels as if tingly currents are running throughout your body. Not only do you get the idea itself, but you understand everything needed to make it happen. And this happens instantaneously.

Life Preserver: A powerful person, group, book, class, hobby, discussion, concept, ideology, or other entity that comes into your life at a pivotal time. This Life Preserver helps save you when you are emotionally drowning or perpetually stuck. A divine idea that resonates with who you really are. A passion being introduced. The right information at the right time. A vehicle for calling your soul back to connection with the Universe.

> "If you don't see a clear path for what you want, sometimes you have to make it yourself."
>
> —MINDY KALING

MISFIT TO TRAILBLAZER MANIFESTO

I am a Misfit. I am an outcast. I've been called many labels that have nothing to do with who I truly am. I wasn't born to be like everyone else. I am here, on the planet, traveling this journey, learning to embrace my true essence. I am here to shed all the messages and programming that said I wasn't acceptable. That I was somehow less than a perfect being of the Universe. Those messages were based on the false gods of ignorance, conformity, and suppression. I witness those false gods perish in the rising light of my own true power. The only acceptance I now seek is my own. I am embracing all of me. I am uncovering all that is irreplaceable about me and declaring it as good! Yes, I am misunderstood. And I no longer wait for others to catch up to my unique genius. They don't get it and they don't need to. I get me. My time for shining is immediately. I stop apologizing for being different. My lifelong love affair with myself begins right now.

I am a Trailblazer. I am a rising phoenix. I am a source of creations only I can make. I wasn't molded to be like everyone else. I wasn't formed to fit. Not only am I "outside the box," I flatten the box and dance on it. I was created to advance civilization forward. To break barriers. To defy expectations. To shatter stereotypes. To demonstrate new possibilities. To give birth to new, sometimes radical, ideas. To be a vessel of overflowing, ever-giving, all-encompassing compassion, kindness, and love—first for myself, right now and always. And once I am fully immersed, thoroughly marinated, ridiculously juicy in compassion, kindness, and love, once they run through my veins and light up my brain, I infect the world with them in a way that only I can. I stand on the rubble of old, vanishing, corrupted systems and break new ground, to lay a sturdy foundation for truth. I am here to envision and birth a new earth, one that works for absolutely everyone, including precious and unique me. I am standing strong for my right to be who I am. To express. To generate. To enliven. To transform. And I'm learning to stand for others too. I am emerging and growing into my distinctive mission. The path is being laid before me, step by step.

I am a Misfit. I am a Trailblazer. Two sides of the same coin. I am here on purpose. I am here for a purpose. And I am embracing the truth of this right now.

_____   _____

Signature   Date

"Too many of us have tried to tone down our weirdness for friends or partners, only to later learn that we were suppressing the best things about us. There's no joy like the joy of being your strange self and finding that there are people who love you for it."

—@SKETCHESBYBOZE (OWL! AT THE LIBRARY ON TWITTER)

1

The Last Picked

**"I THANK EVERY BULLY I EVER HAD
BECAUSE THAT'S THE ONLY REASON
I'M HERE. I LEARNED HOW TO NOT BE
AFFECTED BY IT AND TRIUMPH OVER IT,
AND THAT MADE ME. . . . IF I HAD ANY
SUCCESS WHATSOEVER, IT'S BECAUSE
THESE PEOPLE MADE FUN OF ME."**

—MATTHEW GRAY GUBLER

Did you ever get picked last in school for sports or a group project? Did you often feel neglected by—or, worse, rejected by—others? Maybe this happened in a relationship, while using a dating app, in your workplace, or even by your own family.

When you have a history of being rejected or excluded, it can create a deep need to be chosen, to be included. You might find yourself sitting out on life because you've been waiting for this karmic error to be corrected, for a person to come along and invite you into the action. After all, what you've experienced certainly hasn't been fair. How often we wait for the Universe to even the score, to tip the balance, for justice to reign. You may not even be aware that you are doing this, or that this programming could have been instilled in you oh so many years ago and that you've been waiting to rise ever since.

I'm here to tell you that YOU are the person you've been waiting for.

You can pick yourself and choose where you'd like to be and who you'd like to be around. And that's a much more powerful position to be in than waiting.

Right now, I can guarantee that you know someone who is in a job or relationship simply because they were chosen. Finally! That initial need is met! "They want *me!*" But they never stopped to ask themselves if *they* would choose *them*. I know people who got married simply because a person proposed to them and finally met that need of wanting to be chosen. Of wanting to be wanted. Or started an ill-fitting job because they "won" the interview. As you can imagine, the consequences are disastrous.

I was always the proverbial "last picked for the team" kid. Unless the game was tug-of-war; then fat-kid me was chosen to be the anchor, the last at the end of the line. I remember my face flushing with embarrassment every time a gym teacher said, "Okay, we're going to form teams." A full-body cringe would cause me to shrink and recoil into myself, hoping that if I kept going, I could somehow disappear. I'd start nervously twitching, shaking my leg while staring at the floor. If only I could fast-forward through time and get to the other side, where class was over. Even though I always knew the predictable outcome and tried to mentally prepare myself for it, it somehow never got easier. I would be the last picked, often accompanied by a begrudging eye roll and exasperated sigh. The message was clear. I. Was. Not. Wanted.

In third grade, I found myself with an opportunity to change this, although that had never been the plan. The third-grade teachers brought all three classes together in the gymnasium at the same time. This had never been done before. The partitions came down as the gym was set up with three full volleyball courts. A tournament was about to begin. Our gym teacher explained how this would work: there would be six teams going head-to-head, the winners playing other winners until an eventual overall grand champion was crowned. The PE teacher asked for a show of hands for whoever wanted to become team leaders. My hand rose. This shocked the teachers. It shocked the other students. It also shocked me! I didn't know I was going to do it until my hand was waving in the air. I looked up at it, as if my arm were separate from the rest of me: *What are you doing?* Surprisingly,

I was chosen, along with five other more "usual suspects," the established athletes and popular kids. Everyone was staring at me. One of these things was not like the others. As soon as I was standing before the remaining students, I knew then exactly what I would do. I would pick all the other "last pickeds." I know my people when I see them. My fellow chubby brethren. The kid who came to school in dirty clothes. The shy ones. The girl with the thick glasses. The boy with asthma. Mouths agape, I pointed to each one as they stumbled over to me. Now they were asking, *What are you doing?!* The other five team leaders were visibly thrilled. I had sequestered all the "losers" into one Super Giant Loser team. Just to be clear, I didn't call us "losers"—*they* did, if not with words, then in the way they treated each of us. In this instance, I embraced the word "loser," and in this story I'm using it as a term of endearment and empowerment. They treated us like losers, and they figured I had gotten all of us out of their way. I'm sure they were waiting for us to be the first team eliminated.

Except it didn't work out that way.

As we played, I tried something no one had ever done for me. I supported each of them, unconditionally. Every time a ball was dropped, it stung a tiny bit, much to my surprise. A competitive (and vengeful) spirit had been unleashed inside me and suddenly I wanted more than just not to be shamed. I wanted to WIN! I wanted to show everyone what we could do! All the while, my mind was repeating a common refrain: *That will never happen. Give it up.* For once, I didn't listen. For each teammate, during every mistake, I quickly moved into loving support and kindness. After all, no one *wants* to miss the ball. No one *wants* to hit inside the net. No one *ever* wants to lose. I knew this better than anyone and chose to treat them the way I wish I had been treated. I said to my team members, "That's okay! You got this! Don't give up! There's always another ball coming! You're doing your best! You can do this! I'm so proud of you. You're strong!" I encouraged every single one of them, and the more I cheered them on, the more exhilarated I felt. I put my hand on their shoulders and looked at them until their downcast eyes reluctantly moved up to meet mine. I let them know, "I got you. I'm not ever going to yell at you for making a mistake. *You're wanted here.*"

I'm crying as I'm sharing this now. I saw what was missing, what *I* was missing, and learned to give exactly that. I gave it with enthusiasm and without ceasing. Love poured out of me. I have no idea how eight-year-old me knew to do this. Or how I was wiser (and kinder) than the PE and other teachers. An inner knowing had been activated within and I was speaking and moving from that place. I didn't understand it at all and went with it anyway.

Then the strangest, most inexplicable thing happened. My team started winning! Other teams were being eliminated, one after the other, brought to their knees by our counter-opposite. See, as I had picked all the losers, a super athlete team had formed simultaneously, the other swing of the pendulum. The winners. The jocks. The kids who were always the team leaders. And they were crushing the competition, as they knew they would, as everyone knew they would.

Before I realized it, it was down to just us. Just our two teams. The Winners vs. the Losers. My teammates got very nervous and began fidgeting. After all, across the net were our bullies, our superiors, walking examples of everything we were not. They were the wanted. We were the unwanted. But somehow my anxiety had completely melted away. Feeling loose and unattached to the outcome, I said, "It's okay, guys. All we have to do is try." No one had ever thought we'd get this far. I certainly didn't. I glanced over at the bleachers, at the teachers and other students. Every eye in the room was on us, waiting for us to fall. Waiting for our inevitable failing.

The Winners started out gently, arrogantly, and loudly telling one another to go easy on us. The message was clear. How much they pitied us. How inferior we all were. And how generous and charitable they would be. It only fueled us forward. We rose up, moving as one like synchronized swimmers, and gave it our all! We weren't going to let them walk all over us. No, not this time! When the Winners saw we weren't going to just give up, the air in the gym changed. Quickly, they went on the attack, realizing that somehow we had brought a genuine competition after all. How embarrassing for them! The Mr. Nice Guys façade crumbled as they regrouped. The bad sportsmanship began. There was the intentional spiked ball to my teammate's face, leaving her nose bloodied. She ran to her teacher for help, leaving us down a teammate. The taunting and finger-pointing from the Winners rose like a well-rehearsed chorus. The snickering, snide side jokes, as they doubled over with laughter. One of the Winners blew up his cheeks and bowed his arms out at his sides, mimicking me. Not content to beat us with their obvious athletic prowess, they played dirty. That's what bullies do when their power is threatened. They try to humiliate you back into your place. For the first time ever, I was somehow immune. I could clearly see what was happening, but it didn't sting. Remaining on my same trajectory, I kept it positive, kept encouraging, kept cheering us on. "Look at me! Ignore them! Just stay focused on the ball. Look how far we made it!"

In the end, we lost by one point, coming in second out of the six original teams. The Winners performed a half-hearted bluster of congratulating one another, high-fiving and boasting how they kicked our asses. But their faces said otherwise.

We had decided to stop being what everyone told us we were and take a chance that we were capable of more. We turned away from the hate and moved toward the love. And in love, we broke through our old ideas about ourselves. We may have been the Losers walking in. But every single person in that room knew who the real winners were. It was us! We went from worst to almost first. And we fell in love with one another and had something we'd never experienced in gym class before: fun. It's incredible what our bodies can do

> **"BULLIES WANT TO ABUSE YOU. INSTEAD OF ALLOWING THAT, YOU CAN USE THEM AS YOUR PERSONAL MOTIVATORS. POWER UP AND LET THE BULLY EAT YOUR DUST."**
>
> —NICK VUJICIC

when we encourage instead of shame. Our character was in full view. Along with the character of the Winners. I knew it then. I don't ever want to be them. I don't ever want to put myself above others and abuse them. No, not for me! I want to uplift and inspire. I want to take a stand for love. As I looked around, everyone, including the teachers, was staring at me with an unfamiliar expression. Surprise? Awe? Shock? Horror? Probably a bit of all that. But there was something else, something I hadn't ever seen before. *It was respect.* Funny how that happened when I started respecting myself. I had never walked taller than when I left the gym that day. This place that had been the scene of endless humiliations and indignities became the location of my rebirth. That time when I assembled a team of Davids and we came *this close* to slaying Goliath. The underdogs of my dreams had been born. I was transformed.

Maybe it was always my destiny to be Queen of the Misfits. It's only in sharing this story for the first time that I can see it. All the times I recognized the "different" ones and embraced them. All the times introverted and anxious me was able to forget my usual tendencies long enough to extend a hand to someone who might feel alone and need a friend. All the times I stood up for a person who needed a guardian angel in that moment. Out of my own loneliness, I found ways to create connection with the other Misfits. And out of that connection, out of that love, came an authentic power I could never have expected. This power has fueled a commitment to a life of radical self-acceptance. I go my own way. And I'm head over heels in love with my life and the people in it.

This experience transformed

> **"OUT OF SUFFERING HAVE EMERGED THE STRONGEST SOULS; THE MOST MASSIVE CHARACTERS ARE SEARED WITH SCARS."**
>
> —KAHLIL GIBRAN

me. And it happened because I raised my hand. I got to experience this because I had had enough and thought, "*No*. Not again. Not this time." Because I was willing to lead, or at least a small part of me was. This part took over the rest of me, waving its hand and saying, "Look over here! Me, I want to be a captain!" Even though I had no idea how to lead, let alone how to discard the intimidation and force that had been modeled for me and instead choose love. I just knew I had had enough of being the last picked and being treated like I was worthless. My hand that shot up knew something that the rest of me didn't. That I could choose instead of waiting to be chosen. That I could lead instead of follow. And that I could do it my way. That, yes, this was not only possible, it was possible for me.

The students and clients with whom I work often share their frustration with being on the bottom of "the list." Their kids' and family's lists. Their partner's. Their company's. They are exhausted from being marginalized and taken for granted. How often they wait for this to change, for it to be their turn to be recognized, to feel important, to be embraced, and to shine. They're surprised when I say, "If you're at the bottom of the list, stop putting yourself there." It may seem like this is beyond your control, but no one can place you there without your agreement. And your agreement has most often been communicated in the form of resigned silence. It's completely understandable to be inclined to accept what already feels familiar. This happens out of fear. That compelling fear of rejection, that you will lose what little focus you get, will keep you locked in a pattern of waiting for change instead of creating it. Of counting the crumbs instead of savoring a full, satisfying meal. Our survival mechanism encourages us to give up, submit, and bury our hurt along with our desires.

> ## "IF YOU WANT TO ACHIEVE GREATNESS, STOP ASKING FOR PERMISSION."
>
> —BANKSY

Let me be clear. This doesn't mean you can make someone prioritize you more than they do. If I were able to do that, I'd be rolling in billions right now! However, there is so much that is within your control. You can ask for what you want, negotiate your needs and desires, and set clear boundaries around this. You can then pull back your energy if they are not met, allowing you to get those needs met elsewhere. Perhaps with a person or a company who recognizes your value. Over-giving and under-receiving are often signs of a Misfit. You give, give, give, hoping that others will want you around or that they will finally see how much you matter. Unfortunately, there are far too many opportunists just waiting to take advantage of these fears.

What I am going to say next may seem harsh but I'm encouraging you to let it in. No hero on a white horse is going to stampede in to right the wrong. No one is coming to save you. I know this is difficult to hear. And it's difficult for me to say, even with all that I now know. Everyone who has ever been victimized has fantasized about being saved. These fantasies are a beautiful process to soften the pain from challenging experiences and make them tolerable. It's just that they are, indeed, fantasies, and they can last long after the original wound. These "being rescued" fantasies can keep you stuck, disempowered, and in perpetual yearning. Stopping this cycle can only start with you. And you might not believe this yet, but you absolutely have the ability to do this, to rescue and defend yourself. This power was born within you and can never be taken away. You just need some healing, guidance, and encouragement. That's just what this book was created for.

There's no one more attractive than a person who has claimed their power without apology.

> ## "WHEN YOU'RE BORN TO STAND OUT, YOU WERE NEVER MEANT TO FIT IN."
>
> —JOANNA HUNTER

It's possible the marginalizers have no idea who you really are. Likely, they've been personally benefiting from you not owning your power so it's just more convenient to overlook and label you.

It's going to take courage to do this.

My interpretation of the famous quote below, for our purposes, is that within each of us is a "coward" archetype. This part cowers, acquiesces, and shrivels when being taken advantage of or mistreated. You'll recognize this Coward experience when you are unable to ask for what you want or for a wrong to be righted. You may rehearse what you want to say or do, but when opportunity comes, you just shut down. The Coward quivers with terror and doesn't feel worthy of being heard and seen. I have this inner Coward and you do too.

The Coward experience of being a doormat is a thousand times more painful than standing up for yourself. At least a thousand times more! It will always feel worse than risking a rejection. Standing up for yourself can lead to you being treated fairly and honorably. Every time we cower, we experience a little death that gets repeated and reinforced, over and over again. Please know that there will be people who take notice of this. Being taken advantage of almost never stops on its own, and sadly, it usually increases. With what I know about the nature of energy,

> ## "COWARDS DIE MANY TIMES BEFORE THEIR DEATHS; THE VALIANT NEVER TASTE OF DEATH BUT ONCE."
>
> —WILLIAM SHAKESPEARE, *JULIUS CAESAR*

this makes sense. A pattern of behavior is made of energy, like everything else that exists. And patterns accelerate, continuing in the same direction, until one chooses to disrupt this. Think of Newton's first law of motion, which describes inertia. According to this, a body at rest tends to stay at rest, and a body in motion tends to stay in motion, unless acted on by a force. Being taken advantage of is a pattern of motion until the force that is you acts otherwise. I also believe it's the Universe's way of encouraging you to say, "No, this is not okay." To get clearer about what you don't want so that it can point you in the direction of your true desires. There are times when a situation must become more and more uncomfortable for you to change it. The good news is that along with your Coward, you have an inner Hero too, a champion designed to meet adversity head on. When we empower our inner Hero to stand up, they might not succeed, they might not win, they may even get fired. But that pain is only experienced *once*. And that pain is not just plain pain alone. It's mixed with relief, awe, and healthy inner pride. If you don't access your Hero, you will never know if you could have indeed "won." You will have buried a brilliant opportunity to know this fierce, strong, lovingly protective part of yourself. Don't you want to know that your very existence, one that is more you, can create a different outcome? That you can create a life that brings you from the Misfit you've been labeled as into the Trailblazer you were meant to be?

In my work that I've created called Emotional Alchemy, I teach people how to process emotions and transform how they feel. These principles and practices came organically out of everything I learned in healing the social anxiety that ruled my life for decades. One of the most fascinating truths I uncovered is that my fear of experiencing my painful emotions was far greater than the pain itself. My mind was very convincing that I should stuff down and avoid emotional pain no matter what. But that fear was actually far worse and longer lasting than ignoring this impulse and facing the pain. Much like that death by a thousand cuts.

Here's another truth bomb. One that may land gently.

A time has come for the meek to inherit the earth. Along with the freaks and geeks.

The old ways of aggressive domination and unbridled greed and narcissism are having a profoundly destructive effect on the earth and everyone and everything on it. We see businesses and governments operating with major disregard for the negative consequences of their actions. There is toxic competition happening, where whoever makes the most money, no matter how unethically it is done, "wins." I don't see it as winning if it's hurting people, and you probably don't either.

All of us Misfits were born different to show everyone else how to do things differently. Humanely. Compassionately. Universally. Ethically. Morally. To break the patterns that are causing so much suffering.

> ## "YOU ARE HERE AS THE CREATIVE SOLUTION AND NOW IS YOUR TIME TO SERVE."
>
> —DR. SUE MORTER

Because suffering is an experience we very much understood, we want to do everything in our power to stop it for others.

When you access your Hero and defend yourself, you're not just disrupting a pattern for yourself. You're disrupting an entire paradigm that is gripping tightly to its tired and destructive ways. Its win-lose ways, rather than a new possibility of win-win ways.

You're not an accident or an anomaly. You're very much here on purpose and for a purpose.

Now, you're probably thinking, "What? How can I be in service? How can *I* be a hero? You want me to save the world? I'm still trying to figure out my own life!"

And that's what we all think. I lead an incredibly dynamic life, rich in service to others, rich in alleviating suffering. And guess what? I still think this sometimes.

But please hear this on a deeper level than reactionary fear.

This is *exactly* what you came here to do.

Not to cower before the limited ideas of others!

Not to bow to those who came before you!

Not to live a faint notion of a life you were born into!

And definitely not to sleepwalk through the callings of your spirit.

No, you came here, to this body, to this time in history, to forge a unique path. To see what most can't. To buck the system. To disrupt the old ways and birth the new.

> **"TODAY I REGRET EVERY SINGLE SECOND OF WORRY BACK IN THE UNINFORMED 80s—WONDERING HOW THE WORLD WAS GOING TO TREAT MY BRILLIANT LITTLE BOY WHO LOVED TO TWIRL. LITTLE DID I KNOW THAT HE WAS GOING TO KICK THAT OLD WORLD'S ASS TO THE CURB AND CREATE A BRAND NEW ONE."**
>
> —DEBORAH DIVINE, DAN LEVY'S MOTHER, @TINGTIME

Only you can do it.

And, yes, you can indeed do it!

And I'm not saying this in a "hey, just do it already" way. I'm not a human Nike. It's never that simple. You'll need clarity, practice, guidance, and inspiration. That's exactly what I'm providing here.

In this book, I'm going to share with you how to flip the Misfit coin. Like all coins, there's two sides here. One that you've been familiar with for much of your life: the experience of being different, not fitting in, or feeling like an impostor. There is another side, and that is your inner Trailblazer, who's been itching to rise up in power.

Before you get overwhelmed, consider the best news of all. What you need is already inside you. You were born with it all. My intention is to help you access that power and use it not for just your benefit, but for the benefit of all.

On this journey, you will learn how to:

- *lean into embodying your true essence*
- *heal the Misfit wounds*
- *grow your personal power*
- *manifest the right people and opportunities*
- *agree to lead and like it*
- *feel afraid and still choose to take actions*
- *believe in yourself, even when others don't*
- *give yourself permission to shine*

M2T Journal Moment

Think of a time when you needed rescuing. Write down what was going on at the time, including how you felt.

1. What fantasy did you create for being rescued? (If you didn't have one then, make one up now. Drama fully encouraged!)

2. Write a letter to your Coward. Be incredibly compassionate and kind. Acknowledge their fears and the reason for them. Let them know you're stepping forward to help.

3. Tell your Coward how sorry you are for what they endured. Imagine your Higher Self is addressing everything this part of you went through. Think of everything you experienced that has fed the Coward. What has made you tolerate abuse or go along with anything you didn't agree with? Start with, "I'm so sorry . . ." and fill in the blanks with everything you can think of.

   Examples include: "I'm so sorry you were made fun of in fourth grade." "I'm so sorry you believed when Uncle Henry said you were weird." "I'm so sorry you lost out on the promotion because you were afraid during the presentation."

4. Write out the following affirmations:

   I am the Hero I've been waiting for.

   There is a Hero within me, and I hear its guidance.

   I now stop waiting for anyone to rescue me. I already have everything I need to rescue myself.

   I am worthy of respect, acknowledgment, and consideration.

   I am worthy of being seen.

   I am able to stand up for myself and I am doing that now.

A note on affirmations: These are statements said in the present tense for how you want to feel and what you'd like to believe in the future. Writing them out, repeating them both out loud and mentally, and placing them in your home can help to program your subconscious mind for these beliefs. Get creative in using them in your everyday life. Repeat them while you're on the treadmill, waiting in line at the supermarket, or sitting through a boring meeting. Repetition feeds the affirmations' energy and helps them to manifest in your life. For in-depth information on creating and working with affirmations, see my book *Manifesting* and enjoy the free audio resources that accompany it.

"THE GREATEST ACT OF COURAGE IS TO BE AND OWN ALL OF YOU ARE—WITHOUT APOLOGY, WITHOUT EXCUSES, WITHOUT MASKS TO COVER THE TRUTH OF WHO YOU ARE."

—DEBBIE FORD

2

Famous Misfits
Who Became Trailblazers

"I JUST LOOKED AT THE
PATTERN OF MY LIFE, DECIDED
I DIDN'T LIKE IT, AND CHANGED."

—DAVID SEDARIS

It's easy to look at powerful, accomplished, successful people and believe they just got lucky somehow. To imagine they were always simply beloved, and that eventually that endearment went global. Once a figure is celebrated, it feels only right to imagine that it was always so. How can one fathom that there was a time when the Beatles were considered a long-haired rebellious scourge on youth?! Yet they were. Young people fell in love with them. Their parents and other adults, not so much. (And this was even in the early sixties, when they had the mop-top haircuts!)

There are trends, music, and habits once considered radical that are now so simply mainstream that it's hard to remember they were ever considered weird. As I see hair color of every shade of the rainbow on the heads of everyone from feisty toddlers to even feistier seniors, I too almost forget the days when, to achieve purple hair, I had to use packets of Kool-Aid mixed into a paste and plastered to my head overnight with plastic wrap. You couldn't just buy those kinds of hair colors. That's simply what us weirdos had to resort to "in the olden days"!

Yet when you read biographies and watch interviews and documentaries, common assumptions quickly become dispelled. The sexy singer-songwriter Maxwell only had two girlfriends in high school and didn't go to the prom. Michelle Pfeiffer was ridiculed for the very big lips she's known and envied for. Steven Spielberg was a clarinet-playing nerd in high school. And speaking of band nerds, Lizzo is a classically trained musician specializing in the flute, which she now brilliantly plays for millions of fans. I had never thought I'd see a flute used in pop music. She told the *Hollywood Reporter*, "I chose to be undeniable and I chose to be loud and I chose to be great. And I'm still here." I'm so thrilled she is! (More on her later.) Many celebrities were not the cool or popular

> **"IN A CROWDED MARKETPLACE, FITTING IN IS A FAILURE. IN A BUSY MARKETPLACE, NOT STANDING OUT IS THE SAME AS BEING INVISIBLE."**
>
> —SETH GODIN

kids at all. They were the drama-club drama queens, the out-of-tune guitarist in the battle of the bands, and the geeky coder in the computer room.

There seems to be a journey that Misfits take on their way to becoming successful. It's a journey we can learn from for ourselves. I call this the Misfit to Trailblazer Evolutionary Path.

MISFIT TO TRAILBLAZER EVOLUTIONARY PATH

1. A child is born different in some way and is thus a Misfit.

2. Misfit encounters lack of understanding or, worse, being ostracized.

3. Misfit tries to change themself to be accepted. This doesn't work very well.

4. Misfit as an adolescent experiences a dark night of the soul, a time of

deep existential crisis for which there is no relief. This may include challenging life experiences, like losing a loved one, getting kicked out of school, financial hardship, addiction, or a health challenge.

5. Misfit emerges from the dark night of the soul with a deeper understanding of themselves and decides to embrace who they are and what they're here to do.

6. Misfit is met with more resistance but has cultivated courage through hard experiences and stays true to themself and their vision.

7. Misfit grows in confidence and strength.

8. Misfit starts to get outside acceptance.

9. Misfit is no longer considered a misfit.

> ## "SOCIETY DOES NOT WANT INDIVIDUALS WHO ARE ALERT, KEEN, REVOLUTIONARY, BECAUSE SUCH INDIVIDUALS WILL NOT FIT INTO THE ESTABLISHED SOCIAL PATTERN AND THEY MAY BREAK IT UP. THAT IS WHY SOCIETY SEEKS TO HOLD YOUR MIND IN ITS PATTERN, AND WHY YOUR SO-CALLED EDUCATION ENCOURAGES YOU TO IMITATE, TO FOLLOW, TO CONFORM."
>
> —KRISHNAMURTI

10. Trailblazer is born.

11. Trailblazer advances their area of art or knowledge forward.

12. Trailblazer's gifts become mainstream and accepted.

It's important for Misfits everywhere to recognize this, especially if you're at a stage before 7. For inspiration, I'd like to share a few of my favorites who made it all the way through step 12.

Music M2T Legend: David Bowie

Rock music, by its very nature, is filled with rebels. But even among the most confrontational and creative, David Bowie stands out. I can't think of anyone else who achieved such ever-evolving artistry over so many decades along with the massive popularity he came to achieve, with more than one hundred million albums sold. Not bad for a freak!

As a child, the then David Jones was considered smart but stubborn, always going his own way and frequently getting in trouble for brawling with his peers. This unruly habit caused the injury that would make him look different and then distinctive. At fifteen, fighting with a friend over a girl, his left eye was injured so that the pupil stayed per-

"WHAT I HAVE IS A MALEVOLENT CURIOSITY. THAT'S WHAT DRIVES MY NEED TO WRITE AND WHAT PROBABLY LEADS ME TO LOOK AT THINGS A LITTLE ASKEW. I DO TEND TO TAKE A DIFFERENT PERSPECTIVE FROM MOST PEOPLE."

—DAVID BOWIE

"I SUPPOSE FOR ME AS AN ARTIST IT WASN'T ALWAYS JUST ABOUT EXPRESSING MY WORK; I REALLY WANTED, MORE THAN ANYTHING ELSE, TO CONTRIBUTE IN SOME WAY TO THE CULTURE THAT I WAS LIVING IN. IT JUST SEEMED LIKE A CHALLENGE TO MOVE IT A LITTLE BIT TOWARDS THE WAY I THOUGHT IT MIGHT BE INTERESTING TO GO."

—DAVID BOWIE

manently dilated, which four surgeries could not fix. His family had several members with schizophrenia, including his half-brother and two aunts. This influenced his early recordings. Far from an overnight sensation, Bowie tried many musical avenues that went nowhere. Yet in early recordings of his concerts, you see Bowie performing in front of almost-empty venues as if there were thousands present. He was every bit a successful rock star in his own mind *first*. It was when he finally began performing as his alter egos, like androgynous Ziggy Stardust and later the Thin White Duke, that he became established as a top performer. Throughout his career, Bowie embraced public exploration of many musical genres, along with sexuality, gender, technology, and even business models. When he sang "You've got your mother in a whirl; she's not sure if you're a boy or a girl," from the song "Rebel Rebel," he was bringing visibility, and relatability, to misunderstood misfit young people everywhere. There's something transcendent about seeing another being looking on the outside how you've been feeling on the inside. It gives you courage. It gives you comfort. David Bowie gave this to millions of fans, allowing them to shed the closet and conformity costumes, to strut their stuff. By the time I was introduced to him as a teenager, he had already been influencing the teens who came before me for many years. I found it peculiar that everyone in my high school, and I do mean everyone, seemed to love him, myself included. The drama club kids. My punk rock partners. All my dance-music-loving gay friends. Oddly, even the heavy metal guys. The science geeks. David Bowie followed his inner compass, and enormous success was the surprising result.

Music M2T Upstart: Lizzo

Lizzo is the ultimate M2T transformation unfolding before our very eyes. As a child, Lizzo was picked on for her weight and for being in band. She hid "geeky" interests like playing the flute, anime, and *Sailor Moon* fan fiction. But she decided to turn it all around, to become "cool," and to follow the music she had always loved to wherever it would take her. At one point she decided to own her "bigness," which had been an impediment to getting music-industry attention. As it turned out, she didn't need it. She grew a grassroots fan base that propelled her to stardom.

> "WHEN I WAS A LITTLE GIRL, ALL I WANTED TO SEE WAS ME IN THE MEDIA. SOMEONE FAT LIKE ME, BLACK LIKE ME, BEAUTIFUL LIKE ME. IF I COULD GO BACK AND TELL LITTLE LIZZO SOMETHING, I'D BE LIKE, 'YOU'RE GOING TO SEE THAT PERSON, BUT BITCH, IT'S GOING TO HAVE TO BE YOU.'"
>
> —LIZZO, ACCEPTING HER EMMY AWARD

Boldly taking a radical stand for self-love, which includes hers, mine, and yours too, Lizzo doesn't just speak and sing about it, she creates the actual energy of it. People are actually healed and freed by her and the power of her music! Her love is so big it gets to be received, and reciprocated, by millions.

Art Trailblazer: Andy Warhol

In 1956, Andy Warhol received a rejection letter from the Museum of Modern Art. He had gifted them a painting, for which they said they had no room, and were asking him to retrieve it. It was one of many rejections he would experience in his pre-fame life. Born to parents who emigrated from what is now Slovakia, he struggled with a neurological disorder that caused involuntary movements, and he often missed school. He had other health challenges, like red spotting of the skin, for which he was taunted with nicknames like "Andy the red-nosed Warhola." And there was another big difference as well. Warhol was gay at a time when this was not accepted. He moved to New York after college to pursue his art career and experience more freedom. It must have surprised him when his piece showing two men embracing was excluded from a gallery showing because of the subject matter. Regardless of this and his earlier struggles, he openly embraced his sexuality. Inside the artist was a brilliant entrepreneur and Warhol was able to achieve great success and wealth in his lifetime. Coupling his interests in both celebrities and mass production, he found ways to mass-produce his art of famous friends with silk-screen printings and re-makes of consumer products. I wonder what he would think about how a single drawing or photo can now be shared by millions in minutes. Always pushing

"IF EVERYONE ISN'T BEAUTIFUL, THEN NO ONE IS."

—ANDY WARHOL

himself to try something new, he eventually produced creative works in many areas, including publishing, advertising, film, and music. A survivor of gun violence that left him near death in 1968, he was able to heal and resume working, producing countless works until his death in 1987, years before the internet. Did he have some prophetic knowing when he said, "In the future, everyone will be world-famous for fifteen minutes"? As a kid, I remember thinking, *What does that mean?* Now I see viral videos, personal branding, and influencers, and it all makes so much sense.

Psychology Trailblazer: Bessel van der Kolk

Van der Kolk was born in the Netherlands during the horrors of World War II. Growing up, he was surrounded by Holocaust survivors, seeing firsthand the effects of trauma and PTSD. Finding his way to the United States, he eventually became a Harvard-educated psychiatrist, neuroscientist, researcher, and author. When he became a psychiatrist for a veterans' hospital, working with Vietnam veterans, he was inspired to focus on trauma. (Having early experiences of a painful problem that later gets reactivated, inspiring that person to bring healing to this very topic, is common in a Trailblazer story.) Van der Kolk recognized that trauma was not just present in people returning from the shock of war but in many everyday experiences like abuse. Expanding the definition of trauma to include more sufferers, van der Kolk expanded the reach of services that could treat the biological components of trauma. He found that when a person had undergone a traumatic event, if they had healthy support relationships, there wouldn't be long-lasting symptoms. If a person did not have good support or experienced trauma in isolation, relationships and the ability to experience happiness and joy were severely hindered. The primal aspects of our brain continue to believe that a life-or-death threat is imminent long after it's over. Bringing a deep understanding of how the body holds trauma and how healing relief must be body-centered has changed the entire study and practice of psychology. While

"BENEATH THE SURFACE OF THE PROTECTIVE PARTS OF TRAUMA SURVIVORS THERE EXISTS AN UNDAMAGED ESSENCE, A SELF THAT IS CONFIDENT, CURIOUS, AND CALM, A SELF THAT HAS BEEN SHELTERED FROM DESTRUCTION BY THE VARIOUS PROTECTORS THAT HAVE EMERGED IN THEIR EFFORTS TO ENSURE SURVIVAL. ONCE THOSE PROTECTORS TRUST THAT IT IS SAFE TO SEPARATE, THE SELF WILL SPONTANEOUSLY EMERGE, AND THE PARTS CAN BE ENLISTED IN THE HEALING PROCESS"

—BESSEL A. VAN DER KOLK

explaining that these experiences must be processed rather than suppressed, van der Kolk has studied the healing effects of and encouraged the use of body-centered practices like yoga, altering brain waves via encephalographic feedback, eye-movement desensitization and reprocessing (EMDR), somatic psychotherapies, and EFT, otherwise known as Tapping. His book on this, *The Body Keeps the Score*, came out in 2014 but didn't gather much attention until 2018, when sales took off, peaking in 2021. For more than a year, it was the number-one nonfiction title on the *New York Times* bestseller list, and it has now spent several years on that list. At a crucial time, when people are beginning to understand how past trauma may be affecting their current lives, he offers real hope for long-term healing and relief. Unfortunately, like most Misfits, he has seen his share of resistance to his ideas. But his organic mainstream success has shown how hungry many people are for understanding and healing themselves. This garnered him attention all over the world.

Political Trailblazer Legend: Abraham Lincoln

In our current divisive political landscape, I thought it best to go back to a familiar, famous, and well-loved politician who bucked conventional thought and changed the world. A Republican embraced by people of all parties, he stood up for what he believed in, costing him supporters and

> **"CHARACTER IS LIKE A TREE AND REPUTATION LIKE A SHADOW. THE SHADOW IS WHAT WE THINK OF IT; THE TREE IS THE REAL THING."**
>
> —ABRAHAM LINCOLN

> # "I AM NOT BOUND TO WIN, BUT I AM BOUND TO BE TRUE. I AM NOT BOUND TO SUCCEED, BUT I AM BOUND TO LIVE UP TO WHAT LIGHT I HAVE."
>
> —ABRAHAM LINCOLN

eventually his life. Abraham Lincoln always stood out for his tall, lanky build, earnest faith, and endless curiosity. Everyone agreed that a poet was the most unlikely American president. Forces aligned to have him in the right place at the right time. On January 1, 1863, he signed the Emancipation Proclamation as the nation approached its third destructive year of the Civil War. The proclamation declared "that all persons held as slaves" within the rebellious states "are, and henceforward shall be free." This was a radical and severely opposed act. But it didn't stop him from following what he knew was right, and he blazed a trail for every politician after him.

Spirituality Trailblazer Legend: Shirley MacLaine

There were many people I could have featured here, from Saint Hildegard von Bingen to Paramahansa Yogananda to Martin Luther. It seems the policies of many

> # "THE SOUL IS EVERLASTING, AND ITS LEARNING EXPERIENCE IS LIFETIME AFTER LIFETIME."
>
> —SHIRLEY MACLAINE

modern religions and spiritual teachings do everything in their power to discourage rebellion. At the same time, this area of life inspires exactly that! And many of these teachings were born out of a miraculous experience that went outside of mainstream belief. For the record, Jesus Christ was an unapologetic rebel who loved and spent time with Misfits. He wasn't drawn to perfect people, but to real and humble ones, recognizing there's spiritual strength that can be unleashed through human weaknesses. He also infuriated the government and overturned the tables of the moneylenders, a radical in every sense.

Overwhelmed with possibilities, I kept trying to narrow down the list. Then I was walking through a T.J.Maxx when I kept seeing images of the chakras. There was a figurine sitting in a cross-legged pose with colored dots in a line across it. A similar image was in the framed picture section, the wheels of energy shown in the colors of the rainbow. Next, a book on chakras sat by the journals. All this chakra merch, not in a local yoga studio or new age store, but here of all places. And then I remembered where I first heard of chakras: as a child, watching Shirley MacLaine on *The Tonight Show* with Johnny Carson. It's amazing what the mind remembers after so many years, especially when I

> **"THERE'S NO JOURNEY WORTH TAKING EXCEPT THE JOURNEY THROUGH ONE'S SELF. THAT'S THE MOST IMPORTANT JOURNEY YOU TAKE. I FOUND THAT OUT AS I WENT AROUND THE WORLD MANY TIMES: I WAS LEARNING ABOUT ME."**
>
> —SHIRLEY MACLAINE

had no idea at the time what she was talking about. Shirley placed round-colored stickers on Johnny while he joked nonstop, clearly uncomfortable with the subject matter. A quick YouTube search, and I rewatched the segment from 1983. It was exactly as I remembered it, with her holding her own, no matter how he tried to interrupt and embarrass her. This lady sure has displayed a lifetime of audacity! And there she was, my perfect modern Misfit to Trailblazer Legend for this category.

Shirley was a clumsy child with weak ankles. This encouraged her parents to get her into ballet class, where she flourished for a time before being told—get this—that she had grown too tall and lacked the "ideal body type" because she did not have perfectly constructed feet. (It's common for Misfits to be told early in life that they do not have an essential quality that's impossible to create, like a particular body or body part.) It led her to pursue acting instead, although she danced, and sang, professionally throughout her career. Unlike many Misfits, she found success "accidentally." Early on, as a Broadway understudy, she had to take over for the lead, who had an injury. Soon after, she got a contract with Paramount and became a movie star. Considered quirky and spirited, she forged a highly successful career for decades, eventually writing her first autobiography in 1970.

In her third book, aptly titled *Out on a Limb*, she shared honestly and openly about her esoteric spiritual explorations and how they brought healing to her life. The topics included meditation, reincarnation, quantum physics, unified field theory, astral projection, yoga, channeling, affirmations, and even UFOs. Many of these topics were mostly unknown in Western culture. She opened them up for conversation at a time when many people weren't so sure they wanted to be involved in such "crazy" things. It didn't stop her from shifting worldviews on these "weird" ideas in a massive way. What followed were decades during which Shirley was a national punchline. The comedian Jim McCue said, "Shirley MacLaine will receive Kennedy Center Honors this year. For her career in this and previous lives." This is a kind one. Not many were. She could have backtracked, blaming her interests on mental illness or retreating to a rehab. Or she simply could have disappeared from public life entirely. Instead, she embraced this new role as a new age ambassador and, along with it, the humor too. They couldn't laugh at her if she was in on the joke. She even appeared in the film *Defending Your Life* as the host of the Past Life Pavilion. Of course. It's widely considered that she did much of her best acting after this spiritual public transformation. As of this writing, she continues to both write and act, at the age of eighty-nine.

Because she stepped forward as a spiritual Trailblazer, millions were offered new ways of healing, experiencing, and connecting with the Universe. Much of what was then considered bizarre has been widely normalized. You will see this from the affirmations on a coffee mug to a calming meditation app to the astrology forecasts all over social media. It's all become so integrated into regular life that it's hard to remember how bizarre, and hotly resisted and mocked, it was considered before. You don't have to agree with everything or even anything she believes to admire her courage in risking her reputation and career to be completely, unapologetically, authentically herself. And in so doing, she opened the doors of consciousness itself.

Spirituality M2T Upstart: Vex King

Vex King is someone who has known adversity. Born into a traditional Indian family, Vex's father died when he was six months old. This left his mother struggling to support him and his siblings. There were times they were unhoused and experienced racism and abuse. Always a good student, he did the right thing, growing up to become a successful business-systems analyst. His work brought him into the music business, and his colleagues sought his life advice. Something clicked into place. He found he had answers to share. With a new world opened before him, he began coaching and writing, spreading an online gospel of self-love, positivity, and healthy relationships. He currently has an Instagram following of 1.2 million. Blazing a trail forward with truth bombs, inspiration, and aha moments, Vex is serving a global community with clarity and compassion.

A note on religions: I have the experience of knowing and working with people from any and every conceivable faith, from Judaism to Mormonism to Catholicism and many other forms of Christianity, as well as many types of spiritual teaching. What I am witnessing over and over, within them all, is a conflict between the old ways and the new ways; between the ways things have always been done and the ways they may now be done better; between the continuation of dogma, hierarchies, and rigidity and a yielding to nuance, openness, and flow; between an upholding of current bureaucracy and rules and a return to original meaning and depth.

And I see this revolutionary change reflected in every facet of life as we know it.

For example, within the area of work and career, there has been a huge wave of people who have quit their jobs and are looking for new ways to find meaning in their vocations. Many who learned to work from home during the COVID years decided they'd like to keep working there. New employees are questioning the validity of the forty-hour (more like sixty-plus-hour) workweek and advocating a focus, instead, on completion of tasks. Employers have increasingly let go of employee benefits like retirement accounts, profit sharing, stock options, and tuition reimbursement, leaving employees to ask, How do I get what I need? This lack of security, where employees are not feeling valued or cared for, has led them to look for places where they are.

Our health industry is changing as well. For everyone who has ever been frustrated by the current state of health care, there is a great search under way. From

> **"SELF-LOVE IS THE BALANCE BETWEEN ACCEPTING YOURSELF AS YOU ARE WHILE KNOWING YOU DESERVE BETTER, AND THEN WORKING TOWARDS IT."**
>
> —VEX KING

researching possible causes and solutions for painful conditions to experimenting with self-healing and alternative health techniques, people are looking for more. More relief. More vitality. More energy and youthfulness. Everyone wants to feel better. This has also driven changes to what and how we eat. I, like many, have trouble digesting gluten. I can't tell you the number of people, mostly over the age of seventy, who think this is utter nonsense. "What could possibly be wrong with *bread*?" they ask me. And although I've done any number of things to heal this condition, my body's reactions remain the same. Namely, my face turns the shade of a tomato every time I eat it! It seems the younger the generation, the more and more sensitive, and perhaps food sensitivities are a part of this.

My full-time gig is as an energy coach and healer. I use cutting-edge energy psychology techniques and spiritual practices to help people change how they feel, what they believe, and how to create their best lives. Half of my colleagues who use these same and similar techniques are operating from the more traditional mental health field. They are licensed mental health professionals like social workers, therapists, and psychologists. These professionals are very much blazing a trail by bringing body-centered practices into talk therapy. Some are even designing and conducting studies that are proving the effectiveness of these techniques. There are now hundreds of these studies published in peer-reviewed journals. You see, the fields of mental health and emotional healing have conflicts all their own. Some old-guard mental health professionals are holding tightly to talk therapy as the *only* way to address now-common conditions like depression, anxiety, and OCD. The new body-centered methods for healing nervous system regulation and teaching deep emotional processing for trauma and stress is bringing tremendous relief to those conditions. The old guard will continue to believe it's total quackery. There are times these different perspectives are hotly debated.

What does all of this have to do with going from a Misfit to a Trailblazer? It shows that the old guard is grasping tightly to what has been, for better or worse, while the new way is boldly pushing through, no matter what. It sounds like every generational gap there has ever been. But this feels particularly far-reaching and dramatic right now. The new way is actually not that new, but the old guard has often labeled anything "new" as wrong and dangerous. It takes a while for anything "new" or "different" to be accepted. So take heart—this just means that you are ahead of the curve! You may be here at this time in history to help usher in new ways of governing, healing, or simply being.

Whatever is most ideal will likely build on the old and known while branching out with the new, with the hard-earned lessons and wisdom of the past being carried forward to meet the new creative energies that are emerging. If we want a different future, we need to make changes. I believe each of us is here to usher in fresh solutions.

> **"DON'T WORRY ABOUT NOT FITTING IN. THE THINGS THAT MAKE PEOPLE THINK YOU'RE WEIRD ARE WHAT MAKES YOU YOU, AND THEREFORE YOUR GREATEST STRENGTH."**
>
> —BIRGITTE HJORT SØRENSEN

Here are some of the common qualities in a Misfit to Trailblazer life story:

- *Physical differences that make the person stand out and/or illness or weakness*
- *Childhood adversity with poverty, trauma, abandonment, or abuse*
- *Early independence*
- *Experience being bullied by peers*
- *An inclination to explore and push boundaries*
- *A reputation for being "quirky" or "odd"*
- *Feelings of depression or not belonging, feeling alone or invisible*

- *Interest in things that have not (yet) reached the mainstream, such as certain genres of music, films, books, games, computers, sports, or anything else*

M2T Journal Moment

1. *List a few well-known people you admire here.*

2. *Pick one to research. Look for a moment early in their life when they experienced rejection, adversity, or isolation. Then write down the qualities you believe they must possess to have achieved their dreams (like resilience, strength, a backbone, flexibility, creativity).*

3. *Take those qualities and use them in an affirmation where you claim them as your own.*

   I am sourcing my _____.

   I am learning to be more _____.

   I have _____ and I'm letting it out.

M2T DECREE

Name:

Date:

I vow to:

- learn to accept all parts of who I am
- find the beauty and value in my uniqueness
- check in with myself daily to befriend my feelings
- review my decisions to see whether they are true for me
- be patient with myself on the path of self-love

- place the relationship I have with myself and the <u>Higher Power of My Understanding</u> as a top priority (in place of Higher Power, use the term that works best for you, like the Universe, God, Source, Love, etc.)

- cultivate a sense of safety in my mind, body, and life

- find enjoyable ways to express my true nature

- become open to change

I will no longer:

- apologize for being who I am and how I was created

- waste time explaining myself to people who can't understand me

- wear masks that hide my true essence and light

- exhaust myself trying to win approval from others

- deflect compliments, love, and support

- sacrifice my own needs and desires to prioritize the needs and desires of others

I will use the following to assist in this decree: (examples include journaling, exercises in this book, meditation, prayer, joining or forming a support group, setting boundaries, listening to your intuition, balancing your energy and more)

_____

_____

_____

_____   _____

Signature   Date

3

Finding Your Life Preserver

One thing I've noticed over the years is that life often sends help in the form of what I call a Life Preserver, a chance to be saved from metaphorically drowning. This help doesn't always arrive in the way that you would think, or even in the way you would want (at least, not at first). Yet those Life Preservers keep being thrown your way, again and again, until you're able to catch one and be pulled back to solid ground.

Here's an example of that from my own life that I'm going to call A Punk Rocker Arrives in the Bible Belt.

My freshman year of high school, I was struggling finding people I belonged with. My childhood besties hadn't gone along with my conversion to punk rock (the music, the fashion, the way of life). I got it even then. I had made myself more of a target than ever before. I watched as everyone around me scattered, afraid they'd be sprayed with the shrapnel of humiliation. They didn't get why I had changed, and how could they? My oldest brother, Mike, always a music connoisseur, had consistently commandeered the family stereo that was in the living room. As the seventies gave way to the eighties, the turntable was no longer occupied with New Jersey's native son Bruce Springsteen. There were new and very different tunes on the scene. Whatever he was now playing, I just knew, I wanted more of *that*. There was something in the energy, the vitality, and the power that made my body tingle with tiny explosions. I moved closer to the speakers as if by a will not my own and listened with total focus. The beat. The vibrations. The anger and unapologetic outrage. The truth telling. Here were everyday people, not much older than me, tearing their clothes, spiking their hair, and taking to stages with little musical performing experience. They didn't let anyone tell them who they were. They created themselves. Adopting names like Strummer, Rotten, Vicious, and Scabies (if you know, you know), they took what was considered ugly and repulsive and *embraced* it, celebrated it! I fell in love. These were ultimate outcasts and outsiders who blazed that new trail, and I wanted to come along for the ride. Or another way of saying it: punk rock saved me from drowning.

The Universe always throws you a Life Preserver.

When do you notice your Life Preserver? When you are being ground down by circumstances and feeling utterly forsaken. In the loneliest times of your longest aloneness. When everything seems to be pushing against you, no matter how hard you've been trying to turn yourself around. Those moments of your darkest shame, when you're convinced it will never get better, that you lost out in the life lottery, or maybe have been cursed. When all hope has been cried out.

It's in those moments that something different shows up, big or small, and if you grab hold of it, you will feel that this is just for you. To help you. To guide you. To save you. And it's all very much meant to be. Again, it doesn't always show up in the way or form you would think it will. In fact, much of what or who you think will save you isn't available or able. But the Universe is connected with absolutely everything, so it has countless avenues to get you the right support when you most need it. When you understand that there's mystery and magic in it all, uncovering your Life Preserver is part of the fun.

You see, in those darkest moments that all Misfits have, I believe the Universe is still right there with you. It created you and is within you, so you can never be separated from it. I know that can be difficult to believe when you've been through anything painful. I have had moments myself, more than a few, when I have asked, "Why, why, why did this happen? Where were You?" I've had full tantrums when I've let the Universe have it for seemingly letting me down. It's important to acknowledge and not stifle your feelings in those moments. If you can be honest with yourself and the Universe, you may very well discover what I have learned on my spiritual journey. When I am disliking and criticizing myself, I am pulling myself away from the very support I most need. This is why self-love is so critical in healing, growing, and becoming a Trailblazer. I am known. You are known. I am seen. You are seen. And just like I have, you *will* be shown the way. You just need to grab that ring with both hands when it comes your way.

Now, admittedly, Life Preservers are easy enough to overlook. They can come disguised as an annoyingly well-meaning suggestion from an earnest friend. Or a social event you have zero energy for. That book passed along by your coworker? Or how about overhearing a conversation on a 12-step program? Yep, those can be one too. They mostly fall into a category I call Extraordinary Ordinaries. These Life Preservers look like just another basic experience, one of thousands we encounter in a single day. A song that everyone can hear on the radio, but somehow feels as if it were playing just for you. A book that's been on your shelf for years, which you now feel compelled to take down and read. It seems as if it were written just for you, right at that precise moment in your life. A billboard sign that has a slogan everyone sees as about the product, but it suddenly feels as if it is sending a message directly to you. For example, you're wondering if you can learn a new language when that's been difficult in the past. You see a Samsung billboard that reads "Do What You Can't." I'm not saying that the Universe created the billboard to appear before you in that moment; what I am saying is that when you are ready, anything or anyone can be the messenger that points the way and you'll have an internal experience that is unique. You will be drawn to witness and experience something ordinary, but you will feel it in an extraordinary way. You have the ability to tune in to and receive the answer when you're ready for it. It usually isn't a Disney-movie setting where birds fly down holding banners in their beaks with attention-grabbing music playing in the background. For me, at least, it's usually a headline in an ad in a magazine I'm reading in the dentist's office or dialogue a character speaks in a movie I'm watching. It can be subtle, which is why it's important to pay attention.

Have you already noticed that you've had an Extraordinary Ordinary experience? If so, when you've shared it with others, they might have blinked absently, thinking, "And this is important for you to share because . . . ?" When you explain that the Samsung ad just seemed to scream the answer you'd been waiting for, they think . . . *It was just an ad.* The difference? To them it's just an ad (or a song or a quote), but to you it *feels* extraordinary because it answers an important question, points you in a new direction, or validates something.

The experience is not always songs or headlines or movies. Perhaps one of your friends, the one who always seems to be trying out new spiritual stuff, says, "Hey, I have to tell you about this mindfulness technique I've been experimenting with. It's really helped me focus." (If you haven't experienced this, hold on tight, mindfulness folks are *very* passionate about it. You're bound to encounter this.) As they say it, your mind will likely chime in with what it usually chimes in with. "Oh, here we go again. She always has some magical cure she's pushing. How about you be mindful of my ass! This will be another waste of time." But even as the mind is doing its thing—judging, narrating, cataloging, assuming, and catastrophizing—there's another part of you that makes its presence known. You may hear a vibrating tone in your ear. Like the best ringtone you've never heard. Or an inner knowing that says, "Hmm, pay attention to this." A gut feeling. A resonance. Maybe a dramatic act: a flash of light comes through the window and crosses over your friend's head as she's speaking and circles around to you. Perhaps you feel a vibration through your body as if champagne bubbles are moving through it. Time slows or even freezes. You're in a momentary state of heightened awareness. A supernatural energy has unfurled and made its presence known. It brings an openness that can only inspire intrigue. Your Higher Self is here and starts making the decisions. And that part of you glides right over the doubting, wrestling monkey mind and moves toward *this*. This is what I call the Life Preserver. This is life's gift to you. This Extraordinary Ordinary moment is calling you forward. Grab on and let yourself be saved. Allow that which loves you and created you to pull you out of the turbulent depths and bring you relief.

When you've experienced an Extraordinary Ordinary, hold it close to your heart. You're not crazy. Within a regular moment, something magical has transpired. Take the opportunity.

My first Life Preserver arrived at age eight. I had been moved to a different school for a course called the enrichment program, designed for smart kids. Whereas I had previously been a good student, I was now completely overwhelmed, anxious, and falling behind. A clumsy, chunky, lumbering kid, I had already failed at childhood athletics like jumping rope and playing jacks. I was an ADHD kid before anyone knew what that was, with an auditory processing disorder to boot. While you'd think bringing together a bunch of high-scoring teachers' pets into one classroom would mean safety for all the geeks, it was anything but. We were subjected to constant comparison and competition, which made this highly sensitive girl shut down and shrink into herself more than ever. I was the least smart of the smart kids, all of whom came prepared with outside tutors and homework help. I felt like I was on my own, by now a familiar experience. It was then that my teacher, Ms. Smith, introduced our class to poetry. She read aloud a variety of poems and shared a bit about types of structure. I listened, mesmerized. Then we were let loose to write our own.

Poetry was gentle but revelatory. It also felt oddly familiar, like I'd somehow known about it all along. It wasn't long before I was completely hooked. I loved writing and discovered a gift for rhyme scheme, which I would master by high school. Using pencils and broken crayons to illustrate my original works made it even more exciting. Just in case a piece with a wild title like "Kittens" wasn't clear enough, I took pieces of cardboard and covered them in donated wallpaper samples from our craft area. And Ms. Smith took the pages and sewed them into the covers, creating my first book. Miraculously, I now had a tool. All those big, overwhelming feelings I didn't know what to do with? Here was a place for them in scribbled notepads and composition notebooks stuffed under my bed. On the backs of old envelopes. In letters I wrote to my grandparents. Writing was exactly the right Life Preserver I needed to keep me from drowning. I gripped it to my chest like the salvation it was. I'm still holding it to this day, now as a published author. It all started on that day when Ms. Smith began reading poetry aloud to us. Just look how it saved my life! It was the first of many that would appear just as I needed it. That's why I call them Life Preservers. How would my life have been different if I hadn't recognized that subtle-but-strong connection to poetry that day? Or if I ignored it by deciding it was just homework and not for me?

Which reminds me of an important point: Life Preservers are put in front of you, but you have to actually reach out to grab them.

John Jones
"Best Attitude"

Mary Margaret
"Best Looking"

John Moore
"Most Athletic"

Mary O'Connor
"Biggest Flirt"

Billie NoName
"Most Artistic"

John Smith
"Best Smile"

John Thomas
"Class Clown"

Mary Troy
"Teacher's Pet"

John Walters
"Best Dressed"

A few years later, the punk rock Life Preserver came along at a very important time. I had already become resigned. Having felt shunned in every area of my life, I concluded that this whole living thing wouldn't ever offer much to me. Can you imagine? Already giving up on any happiness in life by age twelve? That's the level of agonizing pain I was in. It seemed like a perfectly sensible solution at the time. Don't aim for much. No dreaming allowed. Just expect a mediocre life and hope it's quiet. No risking being hurt. At least there won't be any disappointment. I settled into a life of complacency. Can you relate to any of those thoughts?

That's when punk rock found me. A self-made world of weirdos where everyone is embraced and allowed to shine as our messy, complicated selves. Anyone could start a band. Anyone? Really, truly *anyone*.

News that my life would be completely uprooted and that I would be moving with my parents to Florida came as a complete shock. My older siblings, Mike and Susan, were long out of the home and established in their own lives. My brother Steve would stay in New Jersey. My Italian grandmother from Pittsburgh would be moving in with us. Life as I had known it, all the comfort of familiarity, would be gone. My home and neighborhood. My church. My school. Everyone I had ever known. While everyday life in Ledgewood hadn't exactly been a paradise, it was home. Still, I had struggled in school with bullies since kindergarten all the way up until I left. In my New Jersey high school, students would yell "Freak!" and "Rughead!" at me in the hallways. I didn't know it at the time, but this was a mild form of what was to come. It had taken all year to get to know the few other resident weirdos, all upperclassmen, and we were finally becoming friends. I just wasn't ready to leave. Figuring out how to take the bus to New York City, while saying I was at a friend's, I had located the legendary CBGB's club. The overwhelming stench of sweat and years of old beer spills greeted me as I walked in. The bathroom was wallpapered with band stickers and graffiti. And more of my kind of people! It was fantastic. Filled with new possibilities, I cried, "I can't go now, just as I'm finding my place!"

There was another worry distressing me, an intuitive hunch that caused my stomach to churn. There was a part of me that knew I wasn't just moving to another state, but another state of mind. That people and beliefs are different in new places. That a student body that hadn't grown up with weird me would be even less tolerant. Looking back, I can see that my intuition was preparing me. Always remember that your intuition is going to guide you; it will point you in the right direction.

Arriving at Tarpon Springs High for the first time, I fell into dread and overwhelm. There were several buildings in an open-campus setting, and my heart was thumping loudly in my ears with anxiety. My mom had encouraged me to tone down my look for the first day. Spiked mohawk was collapsed over to the side. Eyeliner minimized. I put on a normal shirt she had bought me. None of this mattered much, as from the moment I arrived, there was trouble afoot. I could smell it in the classrooms. As I walked the outside halls, scanning the faces, all I saw were glaring sneers and mouths agape. Uh-oh. Where were the artists? Where were the drama and musical theater kids? And the rockers? *Where the hell were my people?!*

Waiting for the school bus, I made an early friend with a New York girl who lived in my complex. She started school the same time I did and we sat together on the very long bus ride, sharing the peculiarities we were each experiencing in our new southern lives. Serafina was of mixed race, tall and stylish, and I wondered why this incredibly beautiful, witty, and smart girl was talking to me. But since she was from New York, she already knew people who looked like me and it didn't faze her one bit. Jointly, we lamented the loss of tristate life (that's New York, New Jersey, and Connecticut) and joked about the hicks and small-mindedness we were encountering. I remember her saying, "What's the whole 'this here' thing about? 'This here pen. This here book.' Don't they understand how stupid that is?" I laughed in agreement since I had been wondering the same thing. But within a couple months, she had moved to a lunch table with the other Black kids, in our self-segregating cafeteria, where everyone stuck with their own. She began taking her own seat on the bus, acting as if we were strangers. I was devastated. I figured that since I had quickly been established as the school pariah, she didn't want any of the crap being thrown my way, both literally and figuratively, to splatter onto her. No one wants to be collateral damage, especially at that age. It's only now, all these years later, that I understand it more fully. We weren't in a place as accepting as New York or New Jersey anymore. As a kid of color in a racist town, she found strength and safety in numbers. She needed to be surrounded by people who were experiencing school in the same way, by people to whom she could relate. Why? So she would be safe. As personal as it felt at the time, looking back I can see that her ending our friendship probably had very little to do with me. And I wasn't capable of understanding her own Misfit journey, a very different one from mine.

Eventually I found my people. Mike was a year older and he and his buddies Chris and Lou were into punk and played in a band. At the end of an assembly, a classmate introduced me to Chris Medina, another chubby punk girl, with big, beautiful black curls and a purple-and-black lace shirt. I was excited to learn she was from New York. We only got to hang out a couple of times before she moved back to the North. We wrote these intensely long letters to each other with "I MISS YOU SOOOOOO MUCH!" in each one. (She's still my beloved friend to this day.) This meant that as soon as people were coming into my life, they were exiting. At one point, even though I'm an introvert, I realized I needed to get proactive. I was missing my siblings and everyone back home. This loneliness wasn't going to fix itself. What was unusual about my school was that there were always new kids starting and almost everyone was from somewhere else. If a kid gave off even a faint hint of oddness, I was set on recruiting them to be part of my crew. Mike told me one day in class, "A new girl started today. From New Jersey. She has an X shaved into her hair." I said, "She's going to be my friend." It took all day until I tracked her down and let her know that there were some cool, open-minded people at this school after all. Stephanie exuded so much beauty and confidence that she didn't need much help from me in making friends, but she joined up with the rest of us anyway. Much like Serafina, I had realized there was strength in numbers. Because even with my new friends, I was getting bullied, and the abuse was growing in severity each day. I dreaded getting on that bus every morning. I never knew if I would be able to open my locker, as someone kept super-gluing the combination lock. Week after week, I'd report this to the school office and they'd send the janitor to use bolt cutters to cut it off. He'd look at me with such pity, like, "Oh, you again." I must have gone through twenty locks. Then there were the phony rumors: that I was gay or a devil worshiper, that I tortured animals or was on drugs. If you see how gay was lumped in with those other three, it will show you just what kind of backward thinking I was dealing with. For them, it was all the same, it was all evil. The funny part is that I was a straight-edge punk rocker, which at the time meant a punk who doesn't drink, smoke, or do drugs. And even though I wasn't gay, I did indeed befriend every gay kid I could find. Although this was the mid-eighties, when Boy George of Culture Club had so many hit songs, ironically, no one was out then. But I had a sixth sense and knew who many of them were. I figured they could use a friend and safe space too. I had always had gay friends since before I knew what being gay even was. I just felt safe and accepted by them and was always happy to reciprocate. Us Misfits are just drawn to each other. Be on the lookout for them. Fellow Misfits are Life Preservers too.

A born-again Christian kid and his buddies kept trying to "save my soul." I'd find "Jesus Saves" stickers plastered to my notes, to my book covers, and even on my back! It was clear he was on a mission, just a misplaced one. I tried to reason with him and explain that I was a really good person, a kind person who dearly loved God, that I'd never hurt anyone. He wasn't buying it. It was my first whiff that the entire nature of religion was very different there, even in a public school. I went to church with my parents every Sunday. In New Jersey we were a practicing Catholic family living in a Catholic neighborhood. And although I had been questioning much of what I had been taught in this traditional religion, I had always had an inner spiritual life. That rested outside of my school experience. What was going on here, twinged with fanaticism, was unrecognizable to me. There was a Christian club at my supposedly secular high school, and Bible verses were invoked in homework assignments. A girl in my math class told me they spoke in tongues at her church. She had to explain it to me four times before I gave up trying to understand. Another told me about his dad's tent revivals, where they used poisonous snakes to test faith. "What is going on here?!" Adding to it were the Scientologists, who seemed to mostly keep to themselves, unless they were quietly slipping me a pamphlet. I kept wondering, *How do the Jewish, Muslim, or atheist students feel about this? Why isn't this school a safe place for all kinds of people?*

There was a growing group who seemed to want to rescue "messed-up" me. To them, I wasn't a real person but a dangerous outsider they could project their labels onto. Some people need to create conflict where none exists. If God is love, then what was going on here, exactly? None of it felt like love, no, not at all. It felt like fear, oppression, hatred, and searing judgment, of a person they didn't even know. All they knew of me was how I dressed. They didn't see the me who saved birds with broken wings. Or the me who came to the defense of anyone being pushed around. There was the me who talked to God as I lay awake each night, struggling to sleep and wondering what I had done wrong. And the me who extended a hand to anyone who might need it. The me who held space for anyone who needed to talk about their feelings, which had happened since I was in first grade. The me who closely guarded secrets and kept confidences. Me? *Was I the problem?* I may not have had the highest self-esteem at that time, but I knew this was dead wrong. If they thought *I* was evil, then I felt anything else they were peddling clearly couldn't be trusted. I knew myself, and others, well enough to grasp this. These experiences and all that followed made me very bitter about God and all religions. I didn't come around to their way of thinking. No, in true rebel form, I threw the proverbial baby out with the bathwater.

Then there was the time I was picked up and thrown into the lockers by a football player. Class was still in session and I had to use the restroom. Running down what I thought was an empty hallway, hall pass grasped in my hand, I suddenly heard footsteps behind me. Just as I turned, I was grabbed and violently thrown, hitting the metal and landing like a motionless puddle on the floor. It happened so quickly that all I saw was the blur of a football jacket while I went into shock. It took a few minutes before I could even think again. Shaking uncontrollably, I limped back to class, and spoke of it to no one. This is common when a person experiences a trauma. Even now, I'm not sure anything would have been done if I had. Speaking up had never made a difference before. Misfits get blamed when they are mistreated, as if our very nature is responsible for creating the misguided or downright abusive behavior of others. Insert "Why can't you be more like_____?" here. Or "If only you were more (or less) _____, then you wouldn't get picked on." Or "You dress that way to draw attention to yourself, then get mad when someone reacts." I'm sure every single adult in that school knew exactly what was happening to me and did nothing to stop it. Some of them likely believed what was being said about me, even while I was writing award-winning essays and scoring stellar grades.

Every day was filled with torment. On the bus, this bruiser used a straw to shoot spitballs into my hair. I landed on my face after I was tripped with a stick. There were the bruises on my arms from punches and pinches. Filled with anxiety, bracing for another attack, I began to fall apart. If there was a God, I thought, then why was he allowing this? Some of it was done in his name, no less! It wasn't the only time I would think, *My God, my God, why hast thou forsaken me?* I had lost my home and town, my friends and church, and now my very safety was in jeopardy on a daily basis.

My sixteenth birthday is a good example of this. I had sunk into a deep depression by then, and whatever faith I had held on to was now thrown away. I spent my birthday in my room crying. My mom presented me with a box from The Limited. This was a store where all the popular girls shopped. In true eighties style, the clothing was bright colors and big shoulder pads, while I was dressing like Wednesday Addams. When I pulled off the lid and looked at this bright yellow sweater set, I was aghast. I looked up at her and back down at it. This was a gift for the teen she *wanted* me to be, not the one I was. This one time, I wasn't capable of pretending. I could not be polite. I handed it back to her and told her to return it. Like all teenage girls, I had been expecting something special for my sweet sixteen. I felt just like Samantha in the movie *Sixteen Candles* (not for the first or last time!). This brings me to an important point. In my parents' defense and the defense of all parents, I need you to know this. Most parents do not want a weird kid, a kid who doesn't fit certain norms or who gets rejected because it's simply too excruciatingly painful for them. Parents want their child to be accepted and "normal" so they will be safe. And let's face it, no one wants to feel embarrassed by their child. A child comes into life with all of their parents' expectations and society's customs placed upon them. There's so much energy put into who they will grow up to be. This is even with the seemingly "normal," non-Misfit kids. There's so much pressure to conform, and those expectations get leveled over and over again. After all, I wasn't alone living in the Bible Belt; there was everyone else who was living there too. I was causing such a stir at school, I'm sure whole towns were talking about it. Although I don't know this for sure, I bet my parents got their share of judgments and snarky remarks. My parents had me later in their lives, so they were about a generation older than my friends' parents. They had a much more old-fashioned value system for me to rebel against. From my perspective, I didn't understand then and don't understand now why anyone cares how another dresses. Again, I knew I was a good person. Why didn't they, and why wasn't that enough? I couldn't understand the constant clashing over my hair and clothes. But it's important to note: life would have been far easier for all of us if I *had* fit in. I do know this. Instead, I was buying fabric remnants and sewing my own clothes, including a prom dress that looked like black patent leather, my mohawk haircut adorned with tiny satin roses. (Wednesday Addams would have been so impressed!) It's clear to me now: I didn't arrive on planet Earth for an easy life but a rich and dynamic one.

More than a genetic mini-me, a child is a unique soul who comes with a soul's mission. That can't be easy on caregivers, and other adults like teachers, who have seen their share of disappointments and the way life works. It's painful to witness someone who is different being bullied, gossiped about, taunted, or excluded. I can guarantee every adult who was in your life as you were growing up witnessed frightening encounters such as these. They may have even experienced some of this themselves. My father was a very large man who also happened to be a dedicated athlete and excellent football player. He told me sports saved him from being ridiculed in school, and it was clear to both of us that that wouldn't be happening in my case. Installed in our driveway was a regulation-height basketball hoop, a smart investment for a family of tall people, I'm sure he thought. But when he spent four hours one sunny afternoon trying to teach me to dribble and shoot only for the ball to sail past the backboard and into the bushes, time and time again, he saw my limitations. No, my M2T story would look much different. He just didn't know that. And at the time, neither did I.

I had my two Life Preservers, writing and punk rock, to get me through. Writing was my healing tool, a place of creative expression, an area in which I could feel healthy pride. Because I had heavy-duty anxiety, writing was also a place where I could express what I couldn't say out loud. Punk rock gave me my crew of sweet and wonderful weirdos, a community of love, acceptance, and safety. We'd record each other mix tapes to share a new band we were salivating over. Then there were the sightings of people like us: "Did you see that guy with the liberty spikes?" Dancing and pogoing at countless rock shows, we met our other Misfits while watching M2Ts on stage. Our heroes were people who had decided to be fully themselves, make their own music, and make their own destiny. There was cannonballing in pools, wandering around the mall for hours, dropping by one another's fast food jobs. We comforted one another through heartache, confusion, and rage. And as much as I felt desperate at the time, to get back to New Jersey, to be close to NYC, to live in a more open-minded place once more, the truth was that we became so incredibly bonded *because* of Florida, not in spite of it. I was a stranger in a strange land, indeed, but I wasn't alone. Because we were so misunderstood, with danger around every corner, it was imperative that we had others to reach for. We couldn't be anonymous, so we needed to look out for one another. Later, when I spent much of my twenties in New York City, I realized that in a place where everyone was different, in which weirdos abound, it was much harder to make true connections. My Life Preservers of community, creativity, and fun continue to this day, decades later. A few times a year, when I visit my family in Florida and spend time with these old friends, the love is still here. That's the thing about Life Preservers: You grab on to keep from drowning in the moment. And some of them keep you afloat for the rest of your life.

My purpose in sharing my story is a few reasons:

I want you to know healing is real. The traumatic experiences and lack of acceptance and support did not prevent me from creating a magnificent life. In fact, many of those experiences caused me to forge my own path that has led to great happiness. I'm sure many who judged me thought I'd end up living like a bridge troll. They could not see who I truly was and am. Everything is healable. *Everything.* What happened to you in the past doesn't have to hold you back now. I promise you: you can heal too and learn to love yourself into a life that sings.

Misfits are made to not be accepted, so we learn how to not cave into social and societal pressure and instead follow our inner guidance.

We are all thrown Life Preservers.

M2T Journal Moment

1. *Think of time in the past or the present where you had/have grown complacent. Where have you given up, numbed out, and accepted less that you deserved or desired? Write about what was/ is happening and your thoughts and feelings that caused this.*

2. *Think of interests and people you really love. Have any of these been Life Preservers? If so, what was going on in your life when they were introduced? How did you feel?*

3. *Looking back on your life, have there been any potential Life Preservers that you may have missed? What happened? Did you talk yourself out of it? How?*

4. *Start an intention to heal the ways in which you may have been impacted by exclusion or bullying. Example: It is my intention to heal from the ways I was hurt in the past. This energy does not serve me. I am willing to heal and allow my true essence to emerge and flourish. I accept all parts of myself now.*

Words carry an energy that gives us information about their most common meaning. How we describe ourselves, as well as how we are described by others, has a very powerful impact on the subconscious mind. Consider the following adverse terms alongside the beneficial terms that are lighter, creative, unique, and likely more accurate alternatives.

ADVERSE TERMS	BENEFICIAL TERMS
Nouns	
Misfit	Trailblazer
Loser	Eccentric
Weirdo	Visionary
Oddball	Nonconformist
Loner	Introvert
Outcast	Vagabond
Wanderer	Adventurer
Outsider	Freethinker
Geek	Techie or Savant or Expert
Adjectives	
Picky	Fastidious
Weird	Eccentric
Freaky	Mysterious
Creepy	Magical
Strange	Creative
Unnatural	Supernatural
Crazy	Kooky
Strange	Offbeat
Bizarre	Remarkable
Odd	Funny
Bizarre	Astounding
Ludicrous	Outlandish
Peculiar	Unique
Nosy	Curious

4

We've Always Been Here: Common M2T Archetypes

M2Ts have indeed always existed, since the beginning of recorded time. I can't say this enough: we are created on purpose for a purpose. Because it's common to feel isolated and alone, I'm exploring some common archetypes here. If you recognize one or more of your particular Misfit-nesses here, it can help you to harness aspects of your growing identity and vision. See if you recognize yourself in one or more of these:

The Rebel
The Whistle-blower
The Fantasy Slayer
The Truth Teller
The Cause Warrior
The Secret Agent
The Paradigm Shifter
The Empath-Mystic

The Rebel

My personal favorite archetype, the Rebel, is here to break out, break down, and then break through what is considered acceptable in loud, often confrontational ways. They're usually sick of how they and/or others have been suppressed and controlled. Defying convention, they tend to express themselves in attention-getting ways.

Rebels are here to wake up everyone around them, to stand for the defenseless, and to be walking examples of courage. The Rebel's gift to us all is that they don't care what other people think! They're most comfortable making other people uncomfortable.

What Rebels need to watch out for is being confrontational for confrontation's sake, rather than for a deeper purpose.

The Whistle-blower

I need to start by saying that no ever one *wants* to be a Whistle-blower. This is an archetype that chooses its person. The Whistle-blower sees or even experiences for themselves injustice or corruption in companies, institutions, and even in families. It begins with a realization that can at times come on quite suddenly. The Whistle-blower is moving along with the accepted protocols when the realization hits—eliciting an unfamiliar feeling that there's dysfunction here, and what was once comfortable no longer is. Or they simply didn't know the practices, policies, and patterns that were in place. Then there is an awakening experience. Perhaps an accident happens in a factory where they work and they witness a deceitful retelling that will prevent spousal benefits for those left behind. Maybe there are hazardous job conditions and a fellow employee tries to form a union, only to see that person's hours cut while being given all of the hardest tasks. Or after losing a parent, the will is being read and suddenly it's made clear that it has been fraudulently changed to exclude everyone but the family member who manipulated it—this happens so often that it's an epidemic, likely on the rise along with dementia. Or their dear friend was sexually assaulted at a fraternity party and they grew frustrated at the college administration that did nothing. The world as they've viewed it has changed dramatically. Less frequently, it's a slower unfolding, a feeling that something isn't quite right, which they push down and do their best to dismiss. There can be very practical reasons for doing this. They believe their employment options are limited or they're on scholarship at school. And let's be real, it's very hard to speak up! There is an enormous amount of risk here, to their social acceptance, their livelihood, and even their lives. And regardless of laws that protect them, I've never seen a situation where there weren't huge personal ramifications for the Whistle-blower, even if the offense they exposed wasn't affecting them. It takes great bravery to bring the darkness into the light. Let us all bless the Whistle-blowers of the world. They must move against that which seems unmovable. It's like there is an awakening and they are able to see with a clarity they haven't before. As much as they wish they could just turn away, they don't. They refuse to go along with a crowd that turns away out of fear or apathy. The Whistle-blowers are able to access great courage within themselves and fight for what's right.

If you're a Whistle-blower, a strong spiritual life is essential. It can be easy to focus on the power of organizations, leaders, and those with more power than you have. But remember, the Universe is the greatest power of all, and you'll greatly benefit from a spiritual support system.

MOVIES ABOUT WHISTLE-BLOWERS

All the President's Men
Erin Brockovich
The Insider
The Inventor: Out for Blood in Silicon Valley
Norma Rae
The Post
Silkwood
Snowden
Spotlight

The Fantasy Slayer

I've been watching with great interest the people who have stepped forward, with enormous courage, to pop the balloons of our collective fantasies. It's a modern phenomena. It seems as if whenever I go online, there's another Fantasy Slayer saying, "Oh, you think this is so beautiful and glamorous? You think this person is so wonderful? Let me show you what's really going on!"

Prince Harry of the British royal family had been viewed as the Rebel for some time, with his teen and young adult antics scrutinized and debated before an ever-critical public. A longtime Misfit, I'm not surprised that he would transform into the Fantasy Slayer, a role that his mother, Princess Diana, modeled for him and that he has since donned, with what seems like reluctance. He married a biracial, divorced American actress. But he didn't stop there. When he and his wife, Meghan Markle, left their royal duties, this caused a great outcry, and plenty of public blaming and shaming for them both. They were interviewed by Oprah. Interviewed! By OPRAH! And during this interview they shared how the royalty business is run. That the royal family is not just a family but an actual business—and run like a cutthroat one—was a revelation. The family is not just complicated, prestigious, and dutiful. Rather, there is an organization that they must answer to that guides their everyday choices and directs the course of their lives. Harry and Meghan revealed in the interview that they were denied mental health care and proper security. Whether you believe them or not, it was clear the purpose of the interview was to inject harsh reality into a royal fantasy cultivated over hundreds of years. Decades earlier, Princess Diana also went to the media, sharing intimate details of her failing marriage and the stress of royal life. As of this writing, Prince Harry's memoir, *Spare*, has debuted, and he does public talks with Dr. Gabor Mate on trauma.

What comes to mind when you think of royalty?

Power and prestige. Elegance and grace. Tradition and stability. Brilliant and beautiful. The adoration of millions. The owners of astonishing wealth. They're special. Extraordinary. Better than regular people. Filled with history and supremacy coursing through their DNA and veins.

I'm not intentionally trying to ruffle the feathers of the British people and other royal fans the world over. Not at all. I'm here to offer what could be an alternative, spiritual perspective: illusions will ultimately crumble so truth can rise to the surface. It would seem that truth always prevails, even if its revelation takes thousands of years. It's very painful to watch a fantasy that's been inspiring or soothing start to crack apart. These losses can be deeply grieved. At the same time, a real love can emerge. A love for real, at times flawed people that is compassionate and understanding.

From a spiritual perspective, we are all children of the Universe, born equal. Often, we elevate other people because we don't feel good about ourselves. When we place other mere mortals on pedestals like they're gods, they are bound to take a tumble. The fantasies aren't healthy for them or the people adoring them.

This doesn't mean you shouldn't look for inspiration in others.

Why Fantasy Slayers Are Important

Sasha's partner contacted me for help. "She literally zones out in a fantasy world all day. It doesn't matter if she's at work or home. Her boss contacted me. It's getting to the point where I can't even have a normal conversation with her and I'm afraid she's going to lose her job!" I understood his frustration. At the same time, I recognized that if Sasha was spending so much time in fantasy, it was meeting a need for relief, just not in a healthy, balanced way. Sasha had always been imaginative, doodling and writing little plays throughout her early schooling. Unusually tall for her age, she stuck out at a time when she would have preferred to be invisible. Kids taunted her with insults and practical jokes. Then she found a simulation game and dove into creating her own online world. Here was the safety and acceptance she had been yearning for! Here she could be bold, sexy, and assertive. Here she could express other parts of her personality, dormant until now. In college, she met her partner and felt true connection for the first time. He felt exactly the same way, having been through his own Misfit adolescence. After college, they quickly moved in together, and it didn't take Sasha long to feel unprepared for life after the honeymoon period. Long-term romantic partnerships and cohabitation can come with challenges. Not having any skills for navigating these difficulties, she turned back to what had given her sweet relief. Her sim-world hours began expanding until they were interfering with real life. When I met with her, she was clear. Her sim life was easy, glamorous, and exciting. Recognizing that it was affecting her employment and relationship, she still found it impossible to stop. Fantasy can be addictive! At the same time, it's like being famished and trading the chance of a delicious meal for a guaranteed photo of one. You're still left hungry. Together we worked on healing the past, developing better communication skills, and cultivating a set of practical skills for decreasing stress, while focusing on all that was going right in her relationship.

If you are relying on fantasy to make a painful life more palatable, please know any relief will be temporary. Ultimately, this practice is doing you a great disservice. Pain exists to get your attention, whether that's a pulled muscle, an annoying job, or a broken heart. Pain is saying, "Something is wrong! Look here." Fantasy is like anesthesia without the imperative lifesaving surgery. Once you wake up, the pain and its cause are still there.

You might be wondering, "But you're a proponent of using visualization to create what you want. Isn't that the same thing as fantasy?" It's important to note that fantasy and visualization are *not* the same thing. If fantasy helped you manifest, every single one of us would be in a perfect love relationship with the celebrity of our choice. Harry Styles, Zendaya, Sydney Sweeney, Regé-Jean Page, and Neil Patrick Harris would each have a few hundred thousand partners. Every teenager would walk arm in arm with their big crush. We'd all be driving our dream cars and vacationing in Tahiti.

It's easy to love a fantasy. After all, they're not real. Fantasy Slayers slash through our collective addictive illusions. This can enable us to embrace the beauty of who we are, who they are, who everyone is, exactly as all of us are. Imagine a time when this is so: loving everyone as they are rather than some contrived perfect version of themselves. That's a world of health. That's a world of freedom. The M2T offers this to everyone. To see that even weirdos are worthy of great love.

The Truth Teller

Since I was a teen living mere minutes from Clearwater, Florida, the home of Scientology, I have been fascinated with cults. How do they start? Why do people join them? How can they follow the rules? What do they get from the cult? It is now widely known that cults are often made up of very intelligent, deeply caring, philanthropic, and extra-hardworking people. How is it that they get caught up in a group that, from the outside, looks bizarre, controlling, or even dangerous?

The answer I found is the same one I've discovered for the "why" of many other misunderstood or dangerous choices. Everyone needs love. It is our greatest motivator, the thing for which we will take great risk. For everyone love-depleted, you see love in places where it is not. Who among us hasn't made a mistake simply because we thought we would be loved?

And now two questions I think each and every one of us needs to ask ourselves: In what ways do I deny my own self because of others? In what ways do I let myself be hurt when I'm seeking love?

Never underestimate the stone-cold power of denial. Denial is the ability of the mind to block the knowledge of what is true, usually because that truth would be painful or shocking. A couple of examples:

A teen girl doesn't know she is pregnant until going into labor. All the normal signs of pregnancy had been present, but out of fear, embarrassment, and shame, she hides this knowledge from herself, until she is doubled over with contractions.

A member on a board of a religious organization thoroughly goes over the financial records and budget. His eyes are drawn over and over again to an expenditure that doesn't seem to have an explanation. But he doesn't ever question it, to himself or anyone else. He never imagines it could be something corrupt. Later, when the religious leader is charged with embezzlement, he is asked, "Why didn't you see this?"

Many cults don't start out with an intention to enslave and abuse members. In fact, many start with very positive intentions for growing a loving community, becoming improved people, and making the world a better place. The problem is, power is so easily corruptible. Right now, we are in a time where abuses of power are being exposed in astonishing numbers. The Me Too movement is a perfect example. What started as a few courageous women sharing their stories of sexual assault and how the assaults were enabled and covered up by others, turned into an avalanche of women from every possible walk of life pushing back against all forms of gender harassment. Interestingly enough, we are simultaneously living in a time when abuses of power are not only exposed but also openly celebrated by fans of the perpetrators, who might be anyone from celebrities to criminals to politicians. This certainly doesn't encourage people to live ethical lives. And any power that goes unquestioned, unchallenged, and unexamined will most likely become parasitic.

This is where the Truth Tellers come in. Either they contain low levels of denial to begin with or their denial gets broken. They see the unwavering, unflattering, and maybe even horrific truth. They recognize the proverbial elephant in the room. An obvious problem is present, so big it's like an elephant. But everyone is pretending it's not there, usually for a good reason. Speaking up will likely cost them in some way. Those elephants have toppled entire companies and governments, brought leaders to their knees. Allowing them to silently stomp around is never healthy. Because the truth is the truth is the truth. No matter of ignoring will ever make anything go away for good. Truth Tellers say it. They put it out there. They literally call it out. This can happen gently and diplomatically. This can be crystal-clear and visceral. That which has been suppressed is brought out into the open.

Example: A marketing company has a meeting to discuss a launch strategy for a client. Much time, effort, and money have already been invested in this approach, and now other employees are being brought in for buy-in. There's an ad presented that may be offensive to a group of people. Everyone sees the offensiveness except the team presenting. An employee raises their hand and says, "This could be misinterpreted in way that is hurtful to a group of people. If we release it, I fear there will be a backlash for this company and for us."

A large family reunion is under way. Cousin Heather is known to have a serious drinking problem. Many previous holidays have been ruined because of this problem. At this event, many family members are drinking in celebration. Heather's speech starts to slur and she loses balance, knocking over and breaking a small statue. Many surround her and coo, "It's okay. You're okay. Don't worry about it." Heather continues to drink and, growing increasingly angry, she loudly accuses her sister of stealing her purse. The Truth Teller, Cousin Carlos, steps in. He says, "Heather, no one stole your purse. You are an alcoholic and need help. You are harming yourself and others. I'm so worried about you. Once you're sober, we will speak about this again and I will get you in touch with resources that can help." The Truth Teller is not met with overwhelming support and relief from everyone present. A few accuse *him* of ruining the reunion. But Carlos knows that love sometimes means saying the difficult things.

Being a Truth Teller can get you in trouble. Telling the truth can cost you friends, jobs, and opportunities. And Truth Tellers are likely not the first on the list for most parties! Yes, telling the truth will make others uncomfortable. And it's almost never comfortable to say it. But we can only heal when what is in the darkness is brought into the light. The elephants are present in the room for a reason.

If you're a Truth Teller, you may have been suppressing what you know because you don't want to hurt anyone. And no one wants to be rejected or ridiculed! This is why Misfits often find themselves in the Truth Teller role. Rejection? We are used it!

Start building your truth telling muscles with others. Practice having difficult conversations with the people in your life. Open up conversations in groups and see how comfortable you can become with differing views. Then practice being radically honest with yourself in your journal. Raise your resilience so when you find yourself needing to say the unsayable, you'll do it with ease.

The Cause Warrior

Oh, how I love these folks! Each and every one of us can thank the Cause Warriors of the world for fighting for justice. They are the leaders of social movements here to push advancement forward. No matter how you feel politically, there are some things almost all of us can agree on. I think most people believe that children shouldn't work long hours in dangerous jobs. But in the 1800s in the United States, this was quite common, for children even as young as seven. This has changed in just a couple of generations. My Italian grandfather came to the United States as a teen and immediately started working in the steel mills of Pittsburgh. This would be unimaginable now. All praise to the Cause Warriors who formed the National Child Labor Committee which turned public opinion around as they fought for protective legislation.

Warriors stand out and are often treated as misfits because they are working on behalf of change. Change is scary. Change is threatening. "What if this change is wrong? What if something bad happens?" There isn't an advancement that has ever existed that wasn't hotly debated and brutally fought. But advance we must. We must do it morally. We must do it energetically.

Buddhists have had this figured out for forever. Everything is impermanent. Nothing stays the same, no matter how hard we try. And each and every one of us, and everything else for that matter, is made of energy. Everything in the entire Universe and the Universe itself are forever in a state of expanding. Not only is the Universe always expanding, scientists now tell us that it is expanding at a faster and faster rate. Evolve we must!

The Cause Warriors, up-front and in charge, can make others uncomfortable. While the rest of us are watching *Ted Lasso* episodes for the tenth time, the Cause Warriors are staying informed, rallying people who feel the same, and pushing forward on issues that matter. They see topics from a new perspective, see a better way to live, and invite new solutions into the global discussion. And they're not going to rest until they've been heard. What they share can be controversial, depending on the company they find themselves in, so they're not always the first invited to the baby shower.

> **"FIRST THEY IGNORE YOU, THEN THEY LAUGH AT YOU, THEN THEY FIGHT YOU, THEN YOU WIN."**
>
> —MAHATMA GANDHI

If you're a Cause Warrior, here are ways to make the journey better for you:

1. Use the internet to spread your message. Just make sure to then get off your phone and into community. Find others who support your message and practice uplifting and supporting one another. The Cause Warrior journey can be chaotic. There will be times you feel overwhelmed and discouraged. With a close team, you can take turns holding one another up when a member gets hopeless. This is the best way to stay strong.

2. Take much-needed time for self-care. The Cause Warrior often feels a relentless sense of urgency. But you'll burn out if you don't slow down and take time for renewal. There's a lot of change waiting to be born. You're in a marathon, not a sprint. Balance the hard stuff with a bit of levity and softness.

MOVIES ABOUT CAUSE WARRIORS

An Inconvenient Truth
Dallas Buyers Club
Food, Inc.
Gandhi
John Q
Roger and Me
Short Term 12

The Secret Agent

Secret Agents, like all the archetypes, have a special purpose. They are able to create change in systems and structures that normally would be averse to giving any other Misfit power. Secret Agents are on a covert mission. They appear to everyone around them as regular people. Their physical presence is disarmingly ordinary. You'd have a very difficult time picking them out of a crowd. Many have the superpower of invisibility. If you've ever worked in a company with an HR (human resources) director, imagine that person. Every HR director I've ever known has a similar appearance. Professional. Calm. Grounded. Wears standard, unassuming, matching outfits. Nothing too creative or flashy. Nothing too memorable. But often they are Secret Agents, or at least the best ones are. There is a reason they operate to serve both the employees and employers. They can get a lot done because they're unthreatening to the status quo. The Secret Agents can introduce positive change in a way none of the other archetypes can. After all, they are running a stealthy operation. The Secret Agent's superpower is making everyone around them feel safe because of their seeming normalcy. And after the power players are ensconced in that safety, the Secret Agent can diplomatically and logically lobby for win-win changes. They don't ruffle feathers. And they rarely receive accolades and glory. Seldomly do they even receive the credit. Usually the power players take that when the changes are a success. No, not the Secret Agents. They just get shit done! If you're not a Secret Agent, then you have known at least one in your lifetime. You just didn't recognize them. You fell for their Clark Kent exterior while ignoring the Superperson inside. I see Secret Agents most often serving in companies of all sizes, local government, social services, school systems, and universities. You might not know that your local librarian, Susie, who extended the open hours, is also a burlesque dancer. George, that administrative assistant who reminds you of character Dwight Schrute from *The Office*? When he's not convincing the boss to close on snowy days, he's leading a cosplay troupe. You'll just never know it. Secret Agents like being a best-kept secret. They recognize how much power that gives them.

> **"WHEN A PARTICULAR MINDSET HAS BECOME THE PREOCCUPATION OF A GROUP OF SCHOLARS IN A PARTICULAR FIELD, THEY ARE SO RELUCTANT TO LET GO OF IT, THEY BECOME EXISTENTIALLY ATTACHED TO IT, AND AN ATTACK ON THE PARADIGM BECOMES AN ATTACK ON THEM, AND THEY VIGOROUSLY DEFEND IT."**
>
> —GRAHAM HANCOCK

The Paradigm Shifter

Always appearing with fresh eyes, Paradigm Shifters arrive into long-established circumstances. Their gift is that they are able to see a new, better, more efficient, or more effective approach that will solve problems. It is all too easy to get stuck in an outdated mind-set. Especially if "this is the way we've always done it" is being expressed. If a person, a team, or an entire field has been following a particular plan of operation, there can be a significant attachment to this. The Paradigm Shifter simply sees differently. They may be a genius at patterns and recognize a dysfunctional aspect, a break in a chain. Or perhaps they are hyperfocused on time management and so bring fresh ways to get tasks done faster.

The Paradigm Shifter can also change an entire field or industry. When the band Nirvana released the album *Nevermind*, the entire music industry was sent into a tailspin. I was a college radio DJ and music director at that time. Our radio station was buried in the back basement corner of the university's student center. As I was walking down the concrete hallway, I heard the first notes of the song "Smells Like Teen Spirit" reverberating against the walls. Instantaneously, it was like bolts of electricity were shooting up my spine! I started walking faster and faster, soon running into the station's lobby, a frequent between-class hangout for the other DJs, to find everyone moving in simultaneous rhythm to the music. This strange knowing came over me. *This* was going to be huge. *This* was going to turn the music industry inside out. Everything would change. And change it did. As the station's music director, I spent parts of my day talking on the phone to people who worked at the record labels. These reps sent us records and CDs, promotional items and concert tickets, to give away on air. They'd try to persuade me to persuade the other DJs to give their artists airtime. In the weeks and months following *Nevermind,* the usual "Hey, what did your DJs think of the new Ned's Atomic Dustbin?" chitchat turned into epic tales of triumph and sorrowful tales of woe. The artists then called alternative were being snatched up by major-label record deals, suddenly holding the power to get mass distribution, airplay, and better tours. These triumphs were not without their own woes as their die-hard fans started accusing them of selling out their indie credibility. On the flipside, the previously megaselling heavy metal "hair" bands died a grisly death. Overnight, their tours were reduced or canceled. Albums shelved in the bargain bins. They became embarrassing late-show punchlines. And this happened so quickly that it left the record companies scrambling to adapt to a change they could not have anticipated. Nirvana ended up being Paradigm Shifters for the rock music industry. Only M2Ts could create music so unique, brazen, and unapologetic that a paradigm shift could happen.

The Empath-Mystic

Sensitives born into an often abrasive world, the Empath-Mystics have a very specific purpose on the earth. They are here to serve as healers, teachers, and living embodiments of a spirit-integrated life, no matter what job title they may hold. Empath-Mystics have a deeper understanding and experience of energy and the unseen world than most. They can often feel the energy in people, places, even inanimate objects. Frequently, they are human lie detectors, as hearing a falsehood sets off an inner knowing, an inner disturbance that sounds an alarm. Many Empath-Mystics have a natural mystical side with powerful gifts, like psychic knowing, mediumship, prophecy, and the ability to explore other dimensions. And every Empath-Mystic I've ever encountered has shared with me how *different* they feel and have always felt. Not many folks know how to react when a three-year-old starts speaking in detail about their past life. Let's bless the parents who see their baby on the monitor giggling with delight to an invisible presence.

Empath-Mystics need community and spiritual mentors.

M2T Journal Moment

1. *Do one or more of the above archetypes resonate with you? Write about how you related to the archetype.*

2. *If they didn't resonate, name an M2T archetype you do feel a connection to. Use your creativity here. There are no wrong answers. Describe how it fits who you are.*

QUICK BIT M2T LIST: POWER PLAYLIST

Here is an era-spanning, genre-defying list of Misfit to Trailblazer songs. To hear this Spotify playlist, visit www.yourdifferenceisyourstrength.com.

Then create your own personal playlist!

Radiohead, "Creep"

Beck, "Loser"

Wheatus, "Teenage Dirtbag"

Katy Perry, "Firework"

The Greatest Showman, "This Is Me"

Frank Sinatra, "My Way"

Sia, "Breathe Me"

Rush, "Tom Sawyer"

Tears for Fears, "Mad World"

4 Non Blondes, "What's Up"

P!nk, "What About Us"

Brandi Carlile, "In My Own Eyes"

Ava Max, "So Am I"

Idina Menzel, "Let It Go"

Bruce Springsteen, "Thunder Road"

David Bowie, "Rock 'n' Roll Suicide" and "Rebel Rebel"

The Shangri-Las, "Leader of the Pack"

Jimmy Eat World, "The Middle"

The Smiths, "How Soon Is Now?"

Against Me, "Thrash Unreal"

Janis Ian, "Society's Child"

Groovie Ghoulies, "Normal (Is a Million Miles Away)"

Joan Jett, "Bad Reputation"

Robyn Hitchcock, "Queen Elvis"

Love in Hate Nation (Original Cast Recording), "The Other One"

Sammy Davis Jr., "I Gotta Be Me"

Sammy Rae and the Friends, "Denim Jacket" and "Jackie Onassis"

Joy Division, "Atmosphere"

The Replacements, "Androgynous"

The Who, "I'm One"

Ben E. King, "I (Who Have Nothing)"

Barry Manilow, "All the Time"

Cher, "Half Breed"

Fame, "Out Here on My Own"

Shirley Bassey, "I Am What I Am"

Pippin (Original Cast Recording), "Corner of the Sky"

Margie Adam, "Best Friend (The Unicorn Song)"

Aimee Mann, "Save Me"

Tori Amos, "Cornflake Girl"

Linda Ronstadt, "Different Drum"

Patti Smith, "Gloria"

Christina Aguilera, "Keep Singing My Song"

Ed Sheeran and Justin Bieber, "I Don't Care"

The Chainsmokers, "Somebody"

Cracker, "I Hate My Generation"

The Clash, "Janie Jones"

Violent Femmes, "Kiss Off"

The Ramones, "Sheena is a Punk Rocker"

Garbage, "Beloved Freak"

Simple Plan, "I'm Just a Kid"

Glee: The Music, Volume 5, "Loser Like Me"

Eric Church, "Mr. Misunderstood"

Gwen Stefani, "Slow Clap"

Kip Moore, "Southpaw"

Papa Roach, "South Paw"

Taylor Swift, "The Outside"

Alicia Keys, "Underdog"

Keith Urban, "Wild Hearts"

Imagine Dragons, "Zero"

Chris Young, "Underdogs"

5

Achilles' Heels and Superpowers

Misfits' Achilles' Heels

When you don't fit in, the pain can be so intense, you'll do just about anything to get the agony to end. Naturally, you'll strive to get acceptance and approval. Those in power, those who are disapproving, hold the key to your acceptance, what you believe will be an end to your loneliness and exclusion. It's inevitable. You become a people pleaser.

People Pleasers and Doormats

People pleasers take cues from others on how to direct their time, energy, money, and other valuable resources. This example of living from the outside in, rather than the inside out, will leave you frustrated, lost, and depleted. And the worst part? The haunting experience of being completely unfulfilled takes up residence in your life. It pervades everything. Because your main motivation is winning the approval of others, you've disconnected from the wisdom of your own soul and who you came here to be. People pleasing will win you a desk full of difficult tasks or weekends overflowing with housework but it will never give you the respect and acceptance you deserve. After all, those in power don't care about you and your feelings; they like taking advantage of you.

They will have less respect for you, not more.

Yes, trying to get that approval means you will be liked less, not more. I wrote about the energy of desperation in my book *Energy Healing*. Our energy fields are always communicating with one another, even when no one is speaking a word. When we feel desperate for another's attention, that is an energy that repels rather than attracts. And while many of us have been the repellents, I can guarantee you've had at least one experience of being the one who is repelled. Think of sales pitches. I feel for anyone working in sales, no matter what they're selling. We've all had so much manipulative marketing shoved down our throats that many of us can smell a sales pitch before it even starts. I remember using a public restroom once and there was a huge ad pasted on the inside door of the bathroom stall. I thought, *Seriously? Is* no place *safe from ads?*

Think back to a time when someone tried to sell you something in which you had zero interest. Maybe they came to your front door. Or you were speaking with a new person at a gathering and you noticed a shift in their voice as they turned the subject into a subtle (or not so subtle) sales pitch. Do you remember that feeling? That twist in your stomach when you recognize, *Ugh, they want my money?* It feels irritating, manipulative, and even invasive. This is the same feeling others can get when you are overly concerned with them liking you.

Here's the most interesting part of this entire scenario. You *think* that you want to be liked and accepted by the insiders. You may have created entire personality profiles about who you believe them to be. Pedestals have been erected in your imagination where they've taken up residence. They are the gatekeepers who have what you want, at least what you've been telling yourself you want. They've got it! The power, the presence, the prestige, the opportunities! Overflowing with cool confidence, everything just goes their way.

Here's what you need to know. It's entirely possible they don't have any of those things. Or not many of them. You've created a story in your mind, a projection placed on them, that may not have much to do with reality.

For some reason, it's just human nature to erect one-dimensional heroes out of three-dimensional, flawed humans. It's very convenient for us to do so. After all, if there are just "superior people," born under an auspicious astrological sign, with the genetic gifts of good looks and vitality, to perfect families with lots of money who provide a top-notch education that opens doors, then why even try? If that's not you, it's easy enough to classify yourself under "inferior people." There's "them" and there's "you." You're on one side of a dividing line and they are on the other.

It's time to erase that line.

All you need to do is look at the children of celebrities, the "nepo babies," to see how off this concept is. Born into "everything" (from a material standpoint), they often lack the motivation for self-inquiry and the hunger to achieve. Frank Sinatra is a perfect example. Born in the gritty, working-class Hoboken, New Jersey, of 1915 to Italian immigrant parents, it's easy to assume that he arrived into the world with a golden voice, a rare gem, a unique gift from the heavens and that his ancestors catapulted him into stardom. That wasn't the case. I was surprised to learn this too. Frank wanted to be a singer, but in his early days on stage he was considered average at best. Strongly encouraged to take voice lessons, he found John Quinlan, an opera singer, who taught him techniques he used for the duration of his career. He *believed* he was a singer, got support, practiced, and honed his craft with dedication, and he became one of the most famous performers who has ever lived. His offspring? Well, not so much. Nancy and Frank Jr. became singers as well, with one hit song between them, while his daughter Tina dabbled in acting, writing, and producing. If what made Frank Sinatra a star was a genetic gift, then you would think his magic or his secret to success would have been shared with at least one of his offspring.

The magic, that X factor, the effervescent light that can draw people and opportunities to us, is available to every single one of us. Not just the genetically gifted. (And most of what we assume is genetics is actually commitment and drive.) Those of us born into less-than-stellar launchpads and with unique dispositions have as much opportunity as everyone else. We just don't seize it. We believe we're not allowed to. We believe that we are what others have perceived us to be.

All those people you're trying to please? They're not as cool, carefree, brilliant, and beautiful as you think. They're as messy as the rest of us. They have disappointments that have never healed and images they're struggling to uphold. Most certainly they have the insecurities that come with the human experience. Those insecurities might not show up in the context in which you know them. For example, your highly confident boss may be an extremely insecure wife or mother. You'll likely never see that side of them.

Doormats take the propensity for people pleasing and let it slide into the darkest dark side. Doormats allow themselves to be taken advantage of, at times in ways that are downright abusive. I know saying "allow themselves" makes it seem like I'm victim blaming here. I promise this is not the case. There are very clear reasons why doormats become doormats, all of them painful. And there's a fine line between taking responsibility for our lives and crossing over into self-blame. Taking responsibility is empowering. Blaming ourselves or feeling blamed by others is disempowering. What I am sharing here is to offer an opportunity to take responsibility for the doormat experience so you can change it. Please know, there are hidden motivations and pain happening within the doormat that makes the entire dynamic unfold. As long as a doormat believes they are a powerless victim, this cannot change. I have known the pain of this experience myself and it's absolutely humiliating. There were a few times in my past where I thought, I will not be able to respect *myself* if I let this continue. There is the pain of feeling like you are in a prison, doomed to live out this life sentence. The hopelessness was far worse because it felt like truth, like this was just "the way it is" and nothing could ever change it. If anyone had come along and said to me, "By the way, you're initiating this," I would have thought them crazy and cruel. But initiating it I was. While believing Misfit me was *inferior*, I drew lots of people who felt *superior*, and they were more than happy to prove this to me again and again.

When you look at the people pleaser and doormat patterns within yourself, I want you to know there are two motivators operating within you:

1. I want to love and be loved, and this is how I can get it.

2. I'm afraid to be harmed, so I must acquiesce.

When you see the motivators, it's easier to be compassionate with yourself about all this. After all, who *doesn't* need to be loved? And who *doesn't* avoid harm? These motivators are true for each and every one of us. But when you're a Misfit, you can experience less love and more harm. So these motivators become overwhelming and desperate. Desperation can lead one to say yes to something they normally wouldn't and prevent one from saying no to anything they obviously should. Even the word "desperate" brings up a level of shame. This descriptive word has now even morphed into an insult. "Ugh, she's so *desperate* in that cutout dress and hair extensions." But where does desperation come from? Unmet needs. That's all. And while our early unmet needs were most often beyond our control, this loss offers a golden opportunity to learn to meet your own needs and to allow the Universe to support you with its infinite resources.

If you had ever met my client Sebastian, you never would have guessed he was a doormat. After a decade building an online business, he was flush with success. Finally, the perfect support staff was in place, his debts were paid, and sales were beyond what he ever expected. He had been working out steadily for a couple of years, cleaned up his post-college diet, and felt strong and healthy. It was the perfect time to marry and start a family. The only problem was his girlfriend, Kiki. As his stability and success had grown, she had relinquished more and more of her own responsibilities. After quitting her job to become an Instagram content creator, she slowly started moving her belongings into his space. Within two months her own apartment was mysteriously gone, and she spent her days on his couch, eating junk food and watching reality shows. This wasn't the "content creation" he had expected. Before long, every household duty was his alone, from laundry to dishes, while he ran the business and paid all the expenses. Whenever he tried to address this, Kiki would explode with anger, throwing things and insulting him. This left Sebastian, a sensitive, thoughtful guy, shaken and discouraged. It reminded him too much of how his mother had treated his father, and he felt like a child again, doing everything possible to calm the monster unleashed in the home. Still, he could not help but repeat the pattern anyway, bringing Kiki flowers, showering her with gifts, all to turn the behavior around. And it only got worse. Days would go by without her speaking to him at all. Here so many areas of his life were better than ever before, and he had never felt worse about himself. By the time he arrived in my practice, he told me he'd do anything to bring the relationship back to the blissful early months of courtship.

I was straight with him. "If I could wave a magic wand and make someone love a client the way they want, I'd be a billionaire right now. No one can do that. I can't change her and neither can you. What I can do is help you heal the pattern that is making you a doormat here. What happens with the relationship afterward will be up to the two of you. At least you will have clarity, high self-esteem, and the ability to make a choice. Because right now you believe you must tolerate this. It feels horrible, but also familiar. Let's heal the past, calm your nervous system, and remind you of who you truly are." Within a matter of months, he ended the relationship. It just happened naturally. He realized he wasn't in love with Kiki, but rather he was in love with the tantalizing possibility of getting her to love him back. Finally accepting his mother for who she was and who she wasn't, he was able to understand and eventually forgive her. He sent me an email two years after we completed our work together. It included a beautiful wedding photo with a woman who was his true partner, both in life and love. Sebastian was a doormat no more!

Silent Sufferers

When I met Prinka, she looked down so often, it was hard to hold her gaze for longer than a second or two. After hearing me being interviewed on a podcast, she had an intense dream, featuring me, of all people. Her dream point of view was outside herself. She witnessed a child version of herself hiding in a cave, holding a shoebox. As she peered inside, she saw an entire town with tiny buildings, roads, and people. I came along in the cave and told her it was safe to come out. When she awoke, she googled pictures of me. After all, she had only *heard* me. My pictures looked the same in real life as in her dream. Already familiar with strange experiences, this was still surprising, and she felt encouraged to contact me. In the first session, I said, "I'm sure you're in the right place, then." But about half an hour in, I was beginning to have my doubts. I have a natural gift for people opening up to me, not just in my work, but everywhere I go. Prinka had such a difficult time telling me anything at all about herself, let alone what she wanted to achieve in our work together. The only clue I had was the dream. I suspected Prinka was what I call a Silent Sufferer, a person who struggles with connecting with the outside world while living in a rich inner one. On a hunch, I asked, "What do you like to do outside of work?" Her head shot straight up, and she became animated as she told me about her gaming. As a video game novice, I asked her to explain what this was about, as it was clearly very important to her. Prinka lived many adventures inhabiting a gaming avatar. She even led her own all-female gaming group. Although many friendships and connections had formed, unfortunately no one lived close enough for her to continue IRL (in real life). (I suspected that if they had lived next door, they still wouldn't have connected in real life.) In the gaming world, Prinka was strong and powerful. She said what she wanted to say when she needed to say it. Concerned with fairness, she made sure the rules of respectful engagement were followed. It was like she was queen of her own kingdom. None of this translated into her regular life, in which she seemed isolated and invisible. Working in IT, she sat at her cubicle all day and didn't speak to anyone, while her free time was spent in character. I told her, "Those same qualities you've cultivated online may be coming from within you. The gaming world feels safe enough for you to explore layers and dimensions of your personality. Don't you want to bring these qualities out and take them for a spin?" Not convinced this was possible, she reluctantly agreed it was a good benchmark to move toward.

Prinka wasn't a Silent Sufferer for no reason. People often describe themselves as shy or introverts and create lives around those labels when they are in fact *scared*. For Prinka, she had been the only student of color in an all-white school. Everything from her name, skin tone, and culture to her grades and vegetarian diet was brutally ridiculed throughout grammar school. This Misfit had a lot of differences to target. Not wanting to worry her parents, Prinka never said anything to them or even to her teachers. She just became more and more inhibited. Books became Mom-approved outlets for relief, escapism, and fun. Later, this transferred to the online world.

Silent Sufferers get humiliated for who they are. They respond by stuffing the pain down and becoming withdrawn, while frozen from asking for support. After all, if you're getting the repeated message that you're inherently bad or wrong, why bother talking to anyone about it? It's just going to bring all that embarrassment up to the surface. You'll believe no amount of intervention will change anything anyway. The effects of this experience can look like depression, loneliness, a life unlived, a voice unspoken, and being lost in alternate realities or addictions.

I suspected Prinka had a powerhouse inside her. We worked together on clearing these old messages out of her energy field. She began to take baby steps asking for support, like help with problem-solving from a coworker and with finding batteries from a store clerk. When people responded kindly and helpfully, she began to see that the world can be a friendly, safe place. For me, it was like watching a flower bloom, as she unfurled before my eyes, able to sit up straight and hold my gaze. We found strategies for bringing her most-coveted gaming qualities out into the rest of her life. I encouraged her to explore and practice with them, to find the ones that were coming from within herself, rather than a performance she was staging. It became very clear that she had natural leadership abilities that eventually found welcome space both at work and home. Approaching her CEO, she asked about beginning a lunchtime meditation session in the conference room, and they enthusiastically agreed. Within a month, anywhere from five to fifteen coworkers would join her there so they could meditate together. This gave her colleagues a chance to finally meet the real Prinka and to get her guidance on this new-for-them practice. Genuine friendships were formed. In her neighborhood, frustrated with increasing vandalism, she formed a neighborhood watch. I chuckle as I imagine this formerly invisible person out patrolling the streets like a badass! Her members meet monthly for a potluck dinner, for which they all hope she'll make her famous saag paneer. While she still has her online gaming, it's now balanced with the rest of her life. She experiences daily a precious, irreplaceable joy. It is the joy of being her true self.

Karma Chameleon

When you don't fit in, you can spend years trying to acquire the ability to do so. After all, the normals have what you don't: acceptance and belonging. This can put you on the perpetual path of delaying your happiness until you get what you want "over there." Being a chameleon is blending in to get outside acceptance.

You witness the soccer stars of grammar school being celebrated after every game. Seeing their swagger and grins as they're showered with compliments gives you a few clues: posture, facial expression, the words being used. Even though you've never been athletic or even followed the sport, you join the team, mimicking what you've witnessed and hoping for the best.

Already an experienced debater, you've created a routine prior to matches that helps you get in the zone. You take a few minutes of alone time and focus on your breathing. That is, until you witness a competing team. Their members all gather in a circle, place their hands in the center, and yell their team's name at the top of their lungs, just like sports teams. Once they win, you decide your prep must be wrong and encourage your team to do the same.

You may be able to fake it for a while, but here's the thing: soon enough someone will be onto you. When anyone is pretending to be something they're not, their energy field is giving off a wonky signal that feels like a disturbance. Imagine a waterfall. When we are being our true selves, the water flows perfectly straight down. When we are pretending to be someone else, it's like huge boulders and tree limbs are blocking the flow, making the water splatter in every direction. It's chaotic and disordered.

Even if you can blend into this adopted role and get the acceptance you crave, you may be shocked to realize that it didn't make you happy after all. Trying to become another person is exhausting. Once you get there, it's even more exhausting to maintain the facade.

Tired of being left out of her workplace's inner circle, Jane decided it was time for a change. After all, this group had banded together and supported one another's projects while hers were repeatedly passed over. She began studying the social media pages of her younger colleagues, discovering their interests and habits. Their lives seemed so glamorous and fun. Creating a playlist of their favorite recording artists, she realized she didn't get this type of music but saw it as a way to connect. Her cyberstalking eventually paid off, and she was flattered to be included in this hip crowd. Jane became a fixture at happy hour gatherings and even weekend hikes. These new friends often sought her advice, like she was an older sibling. But soon enough, she ran out of steam. Bars had never been her scene; the noise was overwhelming. She found herself engaging in conversation on topics that didn't matter to her. These junior colleagues had a great deal of drama in their lives, and she was feeling like a parent to five young adults. And as soon as she thought she was up on the latest whatever, it would change. She couldn't keep up! Jane realized that while she wanted camaraderie and acceptance, this wasn't meeting those needs.

If getting acceptance from others leaves you depleted, it's a good sign you're not being your true self. Shed the cameleon skin and stick to your original, beautiful hue.

Fake It Till You Make It?

You may be asking, but what about "fake it till you make it"? That's another mindset and motivation entirely.

The real you wants to perform in local theater. You've taken an acting class, but your only experience was a play in middle school many years ago. Faking it till you make it will come in handy here. Walking into an audition as if you've been in a hundred plays before will give you a temporary boost so you do go through with it. After all, you don't get good at acting by not acting. It's a skill that needs experience, exposure, and collaboration. Adopt a mindset that you're exactly where you want to be. That's the "faking it" part. Rather than "faking," though, I would call it affirming and envisioning who you want to become. Growing into our dreams needs affirmation and a vision so you know where you're going.

In this example, acting is a genuine desire coming from within, rather than a pursuit to gain acceptance.

Trailblazers' Superpowers

Being Underestimated

While I was writing this section, my neighbors left a present on my welcome mat: a T-shirt emblazed with UNDERESTIMATE ME: THAT'LL BE FUN. And fun it is! They had no idea this is a book topic, but I do!

I've been underestimated my entire life—I'm sure at least partly due to my weight, and mostly due to being different. Our modern ability to make snap judgments of others has become hyperacute. With social media updates and countless headlines flashing before our eyes we are quick to discern. "Yes, I'll read that; no, definitely not that; oh, here she goes again sharing dinner pics—guess what?, no one cares!; skip; skip; skip; skip; he lost weight?, must have had surgery; that new logo is so unprofessional; skip; skip; yes, what about the Spanish Stonehenge?; nope, that's not for me; is she really selling Avon?; oh hell no." While a necessary but not very effective skill in the online world, our rash assessments are often inaccurate impressions in real life.

One of my favorite parts of public speaking is experiencing how differently I am treated before I give a talk versus after. Before, I can be overlooked, ignored, dismissed, or even disrespected. It happens every single time. All I need do is wait. At my moment, I take the stage, unleash my power, channel profound energy, blow the audience's perceptions wide open, then bound down the side steps, radiating elation and relief. Done and done! Then I watch as the now predicable aftermath unfolds. Those very same people are the first to approach me with, "Wow, that was amazing! I mean, just, wow, I wasn't expecting that! Um, yeah, I was distracted before. Hi! Let's exchange cards and keep in touch." While I think it's normal to wish that I were well received and welcomed wherever I go, I've come to a different conclusion from all this: being underestimated is actually a very good thing.

Here's the deal: if they can't see what's coming, they won't get in your way.

One of my clients, Tina, was working as an adjunct professor in a very prestigious art school. Unexpectedly, a permanent, full-time painting professor position became available, and she was quick to apply. Much to her dismay, the college proceeded with a nationwide recruitment to find the best candidate, not knowing they already had her. After all, they wanted a well-known artist, not just a good teacher, and assumed they would have to lure them from a large, cosmopolitan city. Seven candidates were flown in, housed in an extravagant hotel, and wined and dined, all at the school's expense. Tina was sure that they already didn't want her and she could never secure the position. The school knew she was an excellent teacher. Her student evaluation average was five stars. If they had wanted someone like her, wouldn't they have just gone ahead and given her the job? As soon as I heard her say those most familiar words, "someone like me," I knew we had some work to do.

I asked Tina to create a list of assumptions about the seven other candidates. Here's what she said:

1. They come from major cities and have that whole cool vibe.

2. They all have bigger followings than me.

3. They are much better known in the art world than I am.

4. They're all super confident and will sell themselves well.

5. They're all creative geniuses.

Then I asked her to list what she meant when she said "someone like me":

1. I have never lived in a big city.

2. My style of art isn't popular right now.

3. I don't have a big following . . .

Here's where I cut her off. She was essentially giving me the surface information to prove she was the opposite of her competitors.

This wasn't going to be solved in the shallow end of her conscious mind. No, to get to the heart of someone like her, we needed to commune with the child she had been.

I asked her to put one hand on top of the other and place both in the center of her chest. Then I led her through a breathing technique to calm the anxiety response she was feeling. (See instructions on page 120.) As long as her body was flooded with stress hormones, it would be difficult to get to the true heart of the matter.

After she felt calmer, I invited her to imagine she was walking in a place in nature where she felt safe. (The ocean is a common location for this, but not for everyone. A field of wildflowers, a cabin at the foot of a mountain, a snowy hill, a dry desert—there are many possibilities.)

Then I asked her to ask for someone like her to join her there. Within seconds, an inner child or child part who was about five years old appeared on the scene. She had a tattered dress and dirt on her legs and was looking downward with a furrowed brow, as if searching for a lost item. Her shoulders were hunched forward from a heavy backpack.

I helped facilitate a conversation between the two:

> Tina (softly approaching and crouching down): Hello there.
>
> Little Christina (briefly looking up, concerned but slightly curious): Uh, hi?

Tina: I'm here to help. How are you?

Little Christina: Scared. I lost my bracelet. Mommy's going to be so mad. I'm so stupid!

(Here we see that already there is self-criticism. I instructed Tina to gently educate Little Christina.)

Tina: Oh, anyone can lose anything. It happens all the time, to everyone. Stupid has nothing to do with it. I know you're a very smart little girl.

Little Christina: How do you know?

Tina: Because I am you, all grown up, from the future. You don't know this yet, but we're going to do very well in school and eventually become a college teacher. I'm so sorry you're scared. Can I help?

Little Christina (looking relieved): Yes. (She takes Tina's extended hand.)

Tina (looking into her eyes): You are so smart and beautiful. You are such a good girl and I love you so much.

Little Christina begins to cry, and Tina scoops her up in her arms. I ask Tina to bring a healing, colored light into both of them until they are completely enveloped. Tina says all the things her inner child needs to hear. That she is special. Cherished. Loved. How unique and precious she is. Tina even bends over to retrieve the lost bracelet and puts it on her little wrist. Automatically, Christina's dress transforms into a fresh and pretty one. The dirt is gone from her skin and the sparkle has returned to her eyes. When they both feel ready, Little Christina shrinks until she's only an inch big and Tina tucks her into her heart.

When Tina opened her eyes, her face was wet with tears. She now had a deeper understanding of what was operating behind the scenes in the current challenge.

Once she experienced the pain of an inner child who felt stupid and wrong, she saw why she believed her colleagues to be creative geniuses who had all the advantages and she with none. She then admitted to me, "I haven't even seen the art from most of them! I just assumed."

I could have tried to convince her of her worth and intelligence. Asked questions like "How do you know they're all geniuses?" or "Are you sure they all have big followings?" I could have even googled them myself. But if I had used that approach, we would have missed the hurt little girl inside who was influencing a grown Tina. And that little girl was where we needed to focus our efforts. It was she who needed to be healed.

Now that little Christina had been retrieved, acknowledged, and healed, an integration was unfolding between the child part and Tina's current self. A spaciousness was created for grown-up Tina to get her A game going.

I had her script the most ideal outcome for this experience. Basically, she wrote the story of her presenting the best slide show possible and securing the position. (For more details about and examples of scripting, I write more about this in my book *Manifesting*.)

She mapped out everything needed and put extra effort into making it polished.

And her colleague competitors? A few of them, she later learned, weren't even interested in the job. They weren't planning to uproot their already-solid professional and personal lives to move to a place they hadn't wanted to live, prestigious institution calling or not. Flattered by the recruitment, they likely thought, *What the heck, a free trip is a free trip,* but never bothered to put much energy into a compelling presentation.

There was a cocktail meet and greet for the faculty and the candidates. There, Tina quickly surmised who was in it to win it. She used her quiet, unassuming, observant nature to slowly walk in and out of groups clustered in conversation, where the boasting and posturing flooded the room as the liquor flowed. But not for her. Normally, a good gin and tonic would soothe her nerves, but not tonight. She needed a completely clear head and even sharper instinct. None of the other candidates even bothered to give her the once over twice. They had written her off as local talent, not a rock star. At the end of the evening, she didn't see a cool, popular creative genius among them. Instead of sensing their confidence, she felt the arrogance hiding their *own* insecurities.

Enlisting the wheelhouse skills of an eager performing friend, she rehearsed her presentation to get comfortable, adding a couple jokes and vulnerable anecdotes. I advised her to pull together an outfit that both expressed her unique style and made her feel powerful.

Oddly, all candidates were invited to watch the others. She was surprised to find them all lacking. Two candidates took turns insulting one another! She was last to present, which isn't a desirable placement. No one expected what happened next.

Striding boldly to the front of the room, an excitement came over her. In all the healing and planning, she had forgotten how much she *loved* both crafting art and teaching other creatives. It was her true love, her ultimate passion, that which had saved her, and her reason for rising each day. That passion reverberated in every single word. Interspersed with her CV, bio, and art, along with examples of her students' creations, were a few one-minute video testimonials from students. All three had been close to quitting and shared how Tina's instruction, encouragement, and advice had broken through their self-doubt and confusion. It was only then that Tina realized that what she had done for her students, she had just done for herself. Everyone in the room was moved and inspired. Satisfied, she knew she had done her absolute best and risen to this occasion. Regardless of the outcome, she was incredibly proud of herself for how she had healed, prepared, and welcomed this opportunity.

And you guessed it: she got the job!

Not by pretending to be anyone else but by letting more of her true essence shine forth.

After she called me with the sweet news, she said, "I can't believe how I initially thought about this. I had already decided it was never going to happen. I was ready to give up before even starting! I thought you were pushing me to inevitable defeat. And it ended up being a completely different experience. They weren't what I had painted in my mind at all. And neither was I! I'm getting to see more of myself and I'm loving what's here."

If her college had not underestimated her, she would have lost out on the opportunity to slay an inner dragon and rise up to new potential. If her competitor colleagues hadn't done the same, they could have undermined her. The only true competition had been in her own mind. Her inner child, lost in a realm of fear and self-distrust and now healed of feeling stupid, brought back optimistic, childlike enthusiasm and renewed energy.

This story illustrates a few principles about being a Misfit that I'd like to highlight:

1. Become aware of your "somebody like me" or "people like them" dialogues. All of us Misfits have them. During those dialogues, we separate "broken" us from "fortunate" them, reviving old concepts about who we thought or were taught we were, rather than who we truly are. This is where we mentally sabotage ourselves.

2. Become familiar with the dialogue of that old story.

   Recognize what it feels like in your body when you're thinking those thoughts.

   Write down the frequently repeated phrases.

   Rather than avoid the discomfort, meet it with compassion, love, and mercy.

   Then come into the present to who you are now.

Seeing Differently

The greatest gift a Misfit brings to the world is viewing life with all its problems and possible solutions in unexpected, original ways. We see differently. I'm speaking mostly about perspective. Then there is the seeing that can be human in nature, as with some forms of neurodiversity that we're now aware of. A person on the autism spectrum may look at a photo of the New York City skyline and be able to take in hundreds of thousands of minute details the majority would not be aware of. That person could bring a deeper understanding and different view of city planning than a person without that ability.

Because Misfits are drawn to interests outside the mainstream, they bring uncommon knowledge to areas like brainstorming sessions. In just such a session, if eight out of ten people are coming up with the same ideas, it's the other two that bring the most value.

> **"YOU NEVER CHANGE THINGS BY FIGHTING THE EXISTING REALITY. TO CHANGE SOMETHING, BUILD A NEW MODEL THAT MAKES THE EXISTING MODEL OBSOLETE."**
>
> —BUCKMINSTER FULLER

Then there's the importance of inclusion. Mainstream Muggles can stumble in this area simply because they have no idea what it is like to be excluded. I can't tell you the number of marketing campaigns I see where I grab my forehead and say, "Seriously? What are they *thinking*?" What was oblivious to an entire company and the ad agency they hired is instantly, obviously, crystal clear to me. All industries could all use more than a few Misfits to weigh in on such matters, not *just* as experts in diversity and inclusion, where M2Ts clearly dazzle, but in all other areas as well. M2T input is essential. Give everyone a seat at the table. It's a revolutionary invitation for all of us when we see brands like Abercrombie and Fitch lose their power after years of a carefully crafted image of snobbery, exclusivity, and elitism. M2Ts highlighted the horrors and their customers woke up, deciding to put their dollars into brands that are inclusive.

You can bring fresh eyes, honest experience, and a compassionate heart into places where they are very much needed, in ways that others cannot. When you do this, you invite others into your way of thinking. If enough do this, the entire world can change.

Supernatural Seeing (and Hearing, Feeling, and Knowing)

Then there is the type of seeing that is supernatural in origin, that which is beyond normal experiencing, and often mystical in nature. The best way of explaining this is to share examples.

Stepping into your cousin's house, you're greeted by the scent of your mother's perfume. This brings you decades back in time. The last time you were here, she met you at the door with a huge hug. But she's been gone for five years now. As your cousin approaches, you see your mother's image, standing on the staircase, out of the left side of your vision. As you turn to face her, the image disappears. You know her spirit was stopping by to say hello and you feel grateful for the glimpse.

While leaving a shopping center, you feel encompassed by a sense of foreboding. Glancing in all directions, you don't see anything amiss, but you feel drawn to quickly return to the store for something you forgot. Once inside, peering out through the glass doors, you see a speeding car career into the parking lot, lose control, and smash into a section of cars that includes yours. If you had been in or near the car, you most certainly would have been hurt!

Enjoying a rare meal out with an old friend, you listen intently as she shares her desire to move, along with the frustration of not knowing where. While she throws out various locations she's pondering, you see a vision of swaying palm trees and the Walt Disney castle. You say, "Have you considered Florida?" Her mouth drops, stunned. She replies, "It wasn't even on the list, but it keeps coming up! I saw a movie filmed here. The next day I was stuck in traffic, and I couldn't stop staring at the Florida travel billboard. Then I found myself humming along to 'Welcome to Miami' while I was at my mechanic's." Your friend was getting signs from the Universe and used you to further instill the message.

Experiences like this are incredibly common and yet often quickly dismissed. Misfits seem to have a particular propensity for them, so it's important we explore more.

It's my pleasure to introduce you to "the Clairs," along with other mystical gifts.

The Clairs are comprised of four qualities: Clairvoyance, Clairaudience, Clairsentience, and Claircognizance represent supernatural ways of receiving information.

If you're **clairvoyant**, you will see pictures, scenes, or minimovies appear before your eyes. Many describe what they see as similar to the visuals of dreams. Often these images show up as metaphors. For example, you're contemplating leaving your field to start over in a new one and you see a figure climbing slowly, arduously up a steep mountain. It's probably letting you know it's going to be a difficult transition. Or images can be literal, like seeing a section of the parking lot where there is an open spot.

If you're **clairaudient**, you'll hear words or phrases, often giving you deeper insight into a situation. This used to be my least-known Clair. Then one day I just started hearing expressions in client sessions. The voice can be sassy or funny, like when a client shared about taking on a new venture, and I heard, "The dance card is full." As I shared it, we both laughed, because we both know he has a tendency to overload his schedule until he gets burned out. He decided to hold off until he had more bandwidth.

Where are my big feelers at? If you're **clairsentient**, you're able to recognize gut feelings within yourself as well as the feelings and even physical pains of others. A few years ago, I was at St. Paul's Cathedral in London. After an early-morning service ended, I found myself alone exploring this incredible place. At one point, I was behind an altar and felt instantly filled with a grief and sadness that was clearly not my own. I looked down at the floor and in the tiles was a message honoring Americans who died during World War II. It gave me pause to say a prayer before I ventured forth.

You may walk into a hospital or bar and feel a sudden queasy uneasiness. Or your mom calls and before you can answer, you feel a pain in your knee. The same pain she then tells you about!

Claircognizance is the ability to receive what I call "downloads." Rather than seeing just an aspect of a situation, you'll get a complete picture, an all-knowing.

Recently, a new client came to me feeling spiritually blocked. Sarah is Jewish, but her parents raised her as an atheist. It surprised them and herself when she felt drawn to a spiritual path. Having experienced moments of unconditional love and deep connection, she wanted to expand her capacity for this instead of getting shut down. Instantly, I got a download that within her ancestral lines, her family had experienced persecution for their religion. To protect themselves, her grandparents had cut themselves off from their Judaism completely. Sarah's soul had been given the mission to heal this break in her lineage. This entire knowing came through instantly and allowed us to shape our work together to serve this purpose.

Beyond the Clairs are mystical gifts like mediumship, where people are able to connect with or even see people and animals who are no longer living. Or there's the gift of prophecy for those able to predict future events.

In a world now so cut off from its soul and spiritual wisdom, it's incredibly difficult to admit these gifts to ourselves, let alone anyone else. For hundreds of years, people sought spiritual relief in organized religions that provided a framework and guidance for receiving it. Prior to organized religion, people lived in tribes, practicing shamanism. This involved performing rituals and going into non-ordinary reality to receive inspiration and guidance. Modern life has turned its collective back on both organized religion and primal, sacred spirituality. But each and every one of us continues to be a spiritual being, and this will never change. Unless you specifically seek spiritual knowledge and experience, you are an untethered spiritual being, floating without essential guidance to navigate your path. Or you may have been born into a religious or spiritual teaching that judged rather than embraced your spiritual nature. If you have spiritual experiences and no way to understand them, you may believe you're experiencing a mental illness. Or if you share them, another person may think you're consorting with demons, on the extreme end, or simply just doing something wrong. There's so much superstition and fear stifling our innate abilities, like intuition, which every single person has. I believe these spiritual gifts are desperately needed to bring healing to the world right now. Humankind has gotten itself into a whole bunch of jams. The solutions we need will come from a spiritual source and be brought forward by anyone willing to be a vessel for transformation. As a highly sensitive empath, my ability to sense and discern what most would likely call evil, destructive, or just false is advanced as I'm honing my skills daily as an energy healer. I call myself the world's biggest human lie detector. I can practically smell an untruth before it's even spoken. A giant feeler, I can know where congested energy lies in spaces and even in bodies and how to get flow going there. There have been dreams that showed events that later came to pass. Then there's everything I've simply and deeply *known*, without any logical way to have known it. I have never felt these abilities were negative or harmful in any way, not to me or others. In fact, I've used these abilities to help heal myself and now thousands of people. How can anything that brings profound relief, compassion, love, and understanding *ever* be bad?

I believe completely that these abilities are available within all of us. Just like we each have a circulatory system that includes a beating heart, we each have multiple ways of sensing information that would be beneficial for us to know. Like anything out of the ordinary, developing this skill set involves belief that these abilities are real, confidence in your own ability to access them, dissipating any fear, along with study and practice.

Modern life may be partially to blame for these abilities becoming dormant. I suspect in the past, before phones, media, and satellite mapping, people had to rely on these gifts to survive. Some Indigenous cultures that are still around today have members who mostly communicate without words. Whole thoughts are sent and received without speaking, which, if you're living without electricity, is not only necessary but energy efficient. They've always practiced a higher, more natural way of knowing.

For some Misfits, the Clairs come quite naturally. Maybe you saw dead people as a child. Or remembered circumstances from a past life or another dimension. You may be naturally drawn to a spiritual, esoteric, monastic, or mystical life.

If these gifts or interests have intimidated you, I am strongly encouraging you to heal these very healable fears. Our world needs spiritual insight and deeper ways of knowing, now more than ever before. What is confirming this for me are my interactions with young people. I've encountered teens that can do everything, from seeing the moving communication energy of trees to speaking with animals, and yes, seeing dead people. This generation of souls is one powerfully mystical bunch. Within them is also an evolved understanding of emotions and psychology. No matter what age you are, these gifts can be benefitting so many, and they were gifted to you for just that purpose. And no, sadly, not everyone will understand or even just be open. That's a certainty. But within you is the power to experience the haters and doubters, bless them, and keep on going. As you encounter nonsupportive situations, begin to divide people into two categories. The "ones I am here to serve" and the "ones I am not here to serve." The Not Ones can still be your family, friends, coworkers, and teammates; they just won't be spiritual mentors, guides, or the people you'll be helping with your gifts. It's important to have this clarity so you're not discouraged by or judging the folks who just aren't able to comprehend, or are frightened by, otherworldly abilities. If they could understand, they would. If they can't, they can't. It's not at all personal. To serve or not to serve, that is the question.

Independence

There are plenty of people who simply can't be alone. If their schedule isn't full, they will cram togetherness time into every open minute. These people are at a serious disadvantage. Their feeling good or safe is dependent on the participation of others. And others aren't always very effective at helping you feel how you would like to feel. They will struggle with knowing themselves and developing a healthy relationship with the Universe. Those are the two most important relationships in your life and they require alone time. After all, it can be hard to discern where one stops and another begins.

Silence, going within, self-reflection, inquiry, and sacred communion are *internal* experiences. A healthy, balanced life allows alone time *as well as* time spent with others.

You, on the other hand, have independence mastered. If you have ever had a history of being isolated, or at least felt like you were, that seclusion can inspire being comfortable on your own. You've gone through periods of being misunderstood. Maybe even a lot. You've likely had to make friends with yourself because there wasn't anyone else around.

However it was formed, being independent allows you many freedoms, like:

- *the openness to explore alternative lifestyles when it comes to food, work, leisure time, and relationships;*

- *the ability to choose independent thoughts (we are living in a time when conscious and subconscious messaging is everywhere—being apart from the crowd allows you to avoid being influenced by "mob mentality");*

- *the strength to break away from family or community beliefs that don't serve you or your mission;*

- *the capacity to develop a deep relationship with your inner desires (you get important knowledge about what you truly want to have, create, and experience in your life—psst: that's the first step to achieving those desires: knowing);*

- *the opportunity to create time for self-reflection, self-inquiry, the healing of past baggage, and the development of tools for managing stress and processing emotions; and*

- *the space to form wellness and self-care habits.*

When you're not reliant on being surrounded by other people, you can make wiser choices about who you really *do* want to spend time with. People you feel at ease with. People who perceive the true you. Togetherness then can bring depth of connection and sweet, soulful resonance, an opportunity for satisfying emotional intimacy.

(If you've mastered being *too* alone and struggle with building healthy relationships, see the chapter "Finding Your People.")

Creativity

Creativity is not limited to art, acting, music, or writing! Misfits bring a fresh, distinctive, and rare creative essence to everything they do. I've seen everything from using innovative, musical ways of walking to the groundbreaking ideas behind making hybrid plants. Your creative spirit may come out in coding for the web, the way you clean a bathroom, or the tone of voice in which you speak. If you look at the topic of food, you will see countless innovative ways people choose, prepare, and consume food. When you slit an orange wedge and stuff it with chocolate chips then slurp it down in one bite, *that*, dear M2Ts, is a creative act. And one I've witnessed firsthand!

My minister friend Melissa Moorer-Nobles recently shared that in the past she never thought of herself as creative because she wasn't an artist. She now knows that she is the artist of her own life. As are you. I told her, "I'm so glad you don't believe that anymore. It's clearly not true." I knew this easily because of her ensembles. Not outfits, mind you, ensembles. Every time I see her, she is donned from head to toe in the most unique and gorgeous outfits, shoes, and jewelry, put together in a way only an artist could, with beautiful makeup and hair working in harmony with the whole picture. Every day she turns herself into a walking piece of art.

Sometimes the only art I can create in a busy day is my eyeliner!

Our being made different is intentional. We liven up the joint!

And speaking of the arts, while not all Misfits are artists in the classic sense, most artists and other creatives are indeed Misfits. Even those who are well-known and celebrated. Even the seemingly normal ones who look like Martha Stewart. Inside is their Snoop Doggedness, I can assure you. They channel their freakadelic energy into their works and the act of creation itself. When out of apparent nothingness a person brings somethingness, that is the act of a Misfit becoming a Trailblazer.

To create requires courage, independence, free thinking, and a vision. Sound familiar? You're taking a blank wall, canvas, or page and birthing something from you and the ethers that will come through you into that blank space.

Comfort with Adversity

It's popular for modern parents to create lives of great comfort and ease for their children. Most kids these days don't wash the dinner dishes or rake the leaves. Many will not work at a job while still living with their parents. At the same time, they are showered with more material possessions, opportunities, and advantages than ever before. Current corporations have created conveniences for us in ways no people before us have ever experienced. Just look at food. One app and hundreds of prepared foods brought right to your door. And if you want to cook, you don't even have to wash and cut your own vegetables if you don't want to.

> **"THE MOST BEAUTIFUL PEOPLE WE HAVE KNOWN ARE THOSE WHO HAVE KNOWN DEFEAT, KNOWN SUFFERING, KNOWN STRUGGLE, KNOWN LOSS, AND HAVE FOUND THEIR WAY OUT OF THE DEPTHS. THESE PERSONS HAVE AN APPRECIATION, A SENSITIVITY, AND AN UNDERSTANDING OF LIFE THAT FILLS THEM WITH COMPASSION, GENTLENESS, AND A DEEP LOVING CONCERN. BEAUTIFUL PEOPLE DO NOT JUST HAPPEN."**
>
> —ELISABETH KÜBLER-ROSS

Yet when we look at people of renown, universally you see that they have come out of great adversity, not lives of convenience and ease. In the face of challenges and adversity, you have two choices, sink or swim. When you learn to swim, to keep moving, to keep trying, and to create a better life for yourself and others, you develop a resiliency for better managing trials. You don't just expect that everyone you encounter loves and supports you and everything will instantly go your way. No, you remember well the times it hasn't worked that way for you. You just being your sweet Misfit self has brought with it its own adversity. The times you were rejected, excluded and misunderstood. All the times you got the message you weren't okay. Even just the way you feel about yourself can come from a place of adversity if it doesn't align with self-love.

It may be hard to fathom, but this history of personal adversity could very well be your greatest asset. I know this seems impossible. Yet I hope you will hear me out! All life, all growth, all expansion comes with challenges, each and every bit of it. This is *how* we grow, *how* we change. I can be pretty lazy. If I could keep becoming more and more of myself, with all the happiness that results, by laying on the couch, watching Netflix, I would surely do it. But life has brought me many chances to become more and most of them have been wrapped in adversity. Is this surprising to hear from the author of *Manifesting*? Trust me, I know of what I share here. Yes, you absolutely can create a life that sings. In fact, that life is waiting for you. I have, and every day I feel truly, madly, deeply blessed. At the same time, it means you will come face-to-face with unhelpful beliefs, fears of both success and failure, relationship reconfiguring, external pushback, and more. Change, all change, even the very best change, is stressful. No road to a goal is without an occasional block. You have the opportunity to be unfazed by these. You, magical Misfit, have an internal fortitude to keep going, to make it through the dark times until you get to the light. This cannot be given. It is built within you each time you lose, each time you suffer a setback when life does not go your way. It prepares you.

During COVID, there has been a rash of hilarious memes about generational conflict, particularly between millennials and baby boomers. Out of that have come some revelations about the adversity Generation X went through and how it's made us strong. A hilarious meme I saw: "We didn't have playdates when I was a kid. Our parents kicked us out 'til dark. And the weakest among us ended up on Unsolved Mysteries as nature intended." It's a joke, of course, but it demonstrates parental shifts. People who had less comfortable upbringings have developed resiliency, a very good quality to possess! It's important to note that if you've been telling yourself anything along the lines of this: *I can't become who I really want to be because . . .*

> *my parents didn't support me*
> *the school never let me take the classes I needed*
> *I grew up in poverty*
> *no one likes me*
> *I have a disability*
> *everyone thinks I am weird*

. . . or any number of these variations, I implore you to let this story go. You're describing the backstory of almost every success story there has ever been. You're in very good company.

Compassion

Adversity leads us to your next superpower: compassion. People who have suffered become invested in understanding and alleviating the suffering of others. It's no accident that many Misfits become involved in animal rescue, prison ministry, caregiving for special needs children and the elderly, and all other forms of helping make lives better.

Know that beyond being just a feeling, compassion is a vital energy that soothes and heals, both for the giver and receiver.

Often compassion is confused with sympathy and pity. If you feel sorry for someone, or hopeless over another's plight, this is not compassion. Both sympathy and pity have a component of looking down upon and/or judging another, mixed with some hopelessness.

You see an unhoused person sleeping under a highway overpass. Your car is stopped at the light, and you look over, witnessing them stir and awaken, looking bewildered. Your heart aches for such people, so lost in the world, unable to provide for themselves. You stiffen as they approach your car with a cardboard sign asking for money. You manage to stick a few dollars through a slim crack in the window. As the lights turns and you drive off, you're relieved you're not like them.

"COMPASSION CAN BE DESCRIBED AS LETTING OURSELVES BE TOUCHED BY THE VULNERABILITIES AND SUFFERING WITHIN OURSELVES AND ALL BEINGS."

—TARA BRACH

In this example, the person does feel bad for the person they've encountered. But there's a block, a distance, between that person and themselves.

Here's the same circumstance, viewed through the eyes of compassion.

You see the unhoused person and know they must experience great suffering. It's got to be scary and exhausting to live openly on the streets like that. While you've never been without a place to live, you remember that time you got out of the service and couldn't find the right job or location to call home. You had been so frightened and lonely. You take a moment to imagine breathing in and out through the center of your chest, where a gentle warmth begins to awaken and spread. You wave the person over, offer a few dollars and a soft smile, and say, "Take good care of yourself out here. I'll pray for you." As the light changes, you drive off, the warmth inside you multiplied.

Now, in both these scenarios there's no difference in the time taken or money given. The only difference is a movement from the head to the heart, from judging to understanding, from giving fearfully to giving faithfully, from accepting hopelessness to inviting hopefulness.

This is not fakeable. Spreading this level of compassion can only come from deep sincerity. And you, my fellow Misfits, have the ability to expand your natural inclination for compassion and turn it into a healing, life-giving force.

Notice that in this example I didn't create a scenario of weekly volunteering at a soup kitchen or getting a job feeding animals at the shelter. Your compassion may lead you to serve in situations like those and much more. When I speak on compassion, people will share with me that they're waiting until retirement to become a literacy instructor or start a charity. I tell them that isn't what I'm talking about. I'm asking them to feed the compassion in their hearts *right now* and cultivate an innate practice of sharing it wherever they encounter suffering. The frazzled cashier at the supermarket. That little girl crying in the restaurant. A video showing a man narrowly surviving a natural disaster. Yes, even painful situations you see online are opportunities to send compassion, even if you have no direct contact with those involved. These are all places compassion can heal and can heal without you seemingly "doing anything." For the cashier, you send love and peace to them, smile, and conduct the transaction. You don't have to, nor should you, go behind the counter, embracing them in a bear hug! Your compassionate energy is enough of a hug.

Here's how I expanded compassion in my own daily life. I'm someone who thinks everything and everyone should move faster than they do. I just have a naturally fast-acting mind and am prone to impatience and frustration when the situations and people around me don't automatically accelerate in accordance with my will. And I already live in a fast-paced place! Can you imagine what it was like for me when I lived in Florida? When I travel, it usually takes me two full days to slow to the rhythms around me. In the past, this looked like me rolling my eyes, sighing loudly, staring at the car in front, yelling, "Move, you slowpoke, move!" I knew I needed to change this. This was not the kind of energy I wanted to continue putting out into the world.

Here's how I changed this—and how you can too:

1. I recognize the frustration beginning to build.

2. I breathe into my heart space.

3. I start with compassion for myself, for being on a different rhythm than most others.

4. I imagine "that person" who is in my way. Have I ever been "that person"? Have I ever driven too slowly? Sure thing, when I'm unfamiliar with where I am or am passing animals, beautiful trees, or historical architecture.

5. I think of a few possible reasons why "that person" may be driving slowly. An injured right ankle, allergy medication, or a broken heart. (It doesn't matter what is factually happening, which I'll never be able to know, but that I shift my perception so I feel better.)

6. Then I send the compassion out to them.

This has changed so much for me. "That person" is not my enemy, thwarting my fast-paced progress, wasting my precious time! They are my brother, my sister, my person, my friend, just making their way in the world as best they can. It's enabled me to become more comfortable adapting to the pace of life around me. It's for sure made me a safer and more courteous driver. And most of all, I'm putting the kind of energy out into the world that is in alignment with my values and my vocation. Feeling more relaxed, I allow extra time for tasks, feel more present, and thoroughly enjoy them, instead of trying to just get them over with.

There are very simple ways you can grow your compassion and use it to heal every single day. As a Misfit, this superpower will come naturally for you. It just needs a bit of awareness and practice.

Likely it will be easier to feel compassion for others than for yourself. This may seem backward, but I've always found it easier to awaken compassion for others first, then turn it back around for me. When you think about the lack of compassion you've experienced in the past, this makes sense. We can decide what we are worthy of based on how we've been treated, or mistreated, by others. It's time to use this beautiful gift to heal ourselves.

M2T Journal Moment

1. *Recognize which areas you target, when, and how you feel when you are especially unkind to or critical of or even bully yourself.*

2. *Consider the following:*

   <u>Which areas?</u>

   Appearance

   (height, weight, attractiveness, etc.)

   Family

   (divorced parents, dysfunctional family patterns)

   Education

   (certain subjects?)

   Amount of inner brain qualities you possess like intelligence, problem-solving, comprehension

   Achievements (or lack of)

   Work

   Hobby

   Sports

   Relationships

   (family, friends, peers, coworkers, romantic)

   <u>When?</u>

   When others have seen my mistakes or weaknesses

   When I'm with family

When I'm with _____ (specific friend, coworker, etc.)

After I've been on social media

When I'm watching a movie or TV

At a particular time of day (ex. always at night before sleep, as soon as I get up)

How are you feeling before?

How do you feel after you've been unkind to yourself?

1. *Do you recognize in yourself any of the mentioned achilles' heels? If so, which one(s)? Describe a couple of current situations in which you see this in you and your life. If not, is there another Achilles' heel you can think of that does resonate? Give it a title and describe where and how this shows up for you.*

2. *Do you recognize in yourself any of the mentioned superpowers? If so, which one(s)? Describe how you use them now. Then think of a couple ways you can use them more.*

M2T SELF-COMPASSION PRACTICES

1. The HALT Method

This classic exercise comes out of the recovery movement. I have found it can be beneficial for Misfits. Self-criticism *can* feel like an addiction or compulsion because we've turned into our own internalized bully. And long after bullying from others has stopped, you may be still bullying yourself. Finding out what feelings are driving the behavior can be the first step to turning this and other self-destructive behaviors around.

HALT stands for hungry, angry, lonely, tired.

If you're being hard on yourself, HALT and ask these questions:

Am I hungry? If so, what am I hungry for? Food? Affection? Fun? Companionship? Down time? Stability?

Am I angry? If so, what am I angry about? A person, a situation, myself? How can I discharge anger in a safe and healthy way?

Am I lonely? If so, whom can I reach out to? If it feels like there isn't anyone available, how can I befriend and show up for myself?

Am I tired? If so, what can I do to meet this need? Go to bed early? Start eating better and taking supplements? Delegate tasks to another person? Look for a new, less-demanding job?

The self-harshness is pointing you to an unconscious and unmet need. Move from criticism to curiosity and you'll likely silence that harmful inner voice.

HUNGER

Self-harshness is especially unhelpful if you're hungry. Now your blood sugar has dropped in addition to your stewing with embarrassment. Eating a healthful snack will meet the genuine need, serve your body, and prevent you from dropping down a shame spiral.

It's important to be clear about what you're hungry for. It's not always food, and that would be a poor substitute if what you're really craving is joy. Getting clear about your hungers and having strategies ready to meet them can help you be gentler with yourself.

Getting Clear on Hunger

1. What am I really hungry for?

   If it's a food, what temperature (hot, cold, room temp), texture (soft, crunchy, smooth, bumpy), and flavor (salty, sweet, spicy, bland) would most satisfy you?

2. If it's not food, write the ideal situation in which this hunger can be met. Do this *especially* if you believe it's not satisfiable. Like you're hungry for downtime a week before you're taking a bar exam. It's just not possible to take time off in this moment. *Imagine* what it will feel like to have this need met. And make plans for when you can meet this need.

   If it is satisfiable right now, start making it happen!

ANGER

Anger gets a bad rap. It's associated with unruliness and violence, but that's only after it has been suppressed, festers, and explodes, leading to out-of-control actions.

There are no good and bad emotions. There are ones you enjoy having and those you don't, but every emotion has a function. They are giving you vital information, including this one. Anger can be saying to you, "Being treated like this is not okay!" or "I'm tired of always being at the bottom of the list!" or "I have a better way!" When we don't acknowledge and process our anger, it's easy enough to use it against ourselves. In fact, there are many that define depression as anger turned inward. Self-criticism, insults, mocking, minimizing, and pushing are all ways your anger harms yourself. You've had enough of that from others. Let's turn this around.

> "Boundaries are the distance at which I can love you and me simultaneously."
>
> —PRENTICE HEMPHILL

Getting Clarity on Anger

1. Ask your anger what it wants you to know. Give it a voice, write it down, uncensored.

2. What actions can you take to change these circumstances? Be open to new possibilities here.

3. What boundaries can you set?

4. With the insights you've uncovered in this exercise, practice saying no, setting limits, establishing boundaries in writing here. Now that you've gotten the message, it's the perfect time to process it.

For much of my teens and twenties, anger was the only emotion I experienced. I got angry when life didn't go my way. I was furious with how I was mistreated. Frustrated when the supermarket was out of peaches, I'd seethe all the way home. Stewing in resentment, it didn't much matter what was happening. This means I know both how destructive it can be and I've gotten really good at learning how to process it and showing others how to do the same.

Ways to Process the Energy of Anger

1. Move your body. Anger isn't in your head. It's in your entire being. That stuck energy needs to flow through and out of you. Just work *with* rather than *against* your body by not hurting yourself physically in the process. Honor any physical limitations and do what you are able.

2. Get a cheap, lightweight, plastic Wiffle ball–type bat. Get in touch with the anger you're feeling and smash the bat onto a pile of pillows, laundry, your couch, or mattress. Anything soft that has a give to it will work. Imagine you are pulling the anger up, down your arms, and out through the tip of the bat, expelling your anger each time your arms thrust forward.

> *This is one my personal favorites. I'll never forget how the basement had flooded right after I moved into my then house, indicating a history that hadn't been disclosed. One night, in my room, while wearing a giant neon-orange bathrobe and green face mask, I knew I had to get the anger out as to not ruin my new joy of home ownership. I found my Anger Bat (I call her Ramona) in a box and started whacking away on my old couch, using every known obscenity. That is, until I heard a loud gasp. I looked up, out of the uncovered windows, to see a teen boy frozen on the sidewalk, just a few feet away. It's then that I saw my reflection along with the look of absolute horror on his face! I started to laugh, big belly laughs, and couldn't stop! What can I say, that neighborhood was never the same. I sure make an entrance! And I felt incredible afterward.*

3. Break some stuff. Take a hammer to that old trophy, your ex's champagne flutes, that cheap vase destined for recycling. Visit a rage room.

4. Hold an intention to expel the anger. Then scream at the top of your lungs until there's nothing left. Punch your arms in the air while doing it. Getting out into the woods is ideal for this one.

5. Try this exercise. Stand with your feet in a wide stance, toes turned slightly out. Raise your arms up in the air in a V formation. Breathe in deeply through the nose

and, as you exhale through the mouth, drop into a squat and sweep your arms down and back. Again, work with your body on this.

LONELINESS

Loneliness can show up in every circumstance, including when you are with people. This is especially true for Misfits since we get reminded of the differences between us and others. So getting into a crowd isn't necessarily going to cut it. You're seeking true connection with another who accepts you and feels comfortable with who you are. Just don't expect them to know what you need unless you learn to ask for it.

Call a friend, family, or another loved one. Be vulnerable, open up, be honest, and say, "I'm feeling lonely right now." Follow up with what you need. Make it clear and specific. "Can you chat with me while I make dinner?" or "Do you have a few minutes so I can tell you what's happening?" or "Can we get together this weekend to meet for coffee?"

If you don't have anyone like this in your life right now, or even if you do, here's a couple other options:

Support Groups

1. There are twelve-step groups for every addiction and Al-Anon to support the friends and family of people with addiction. You may be surprised to learn you do not have to have an addiction to benefit from doing the twelve steps themselves. These groups also happen to be incredible examples of supportive community, where you can get a sponsor to guide and be there for you, no matter what.

2. Then there are groups for grief, PTSD (ideal for anyone bullied), domestic violence, disabilities, and medical diagnoses like cancer. Most schools and colleges have peer support groups where everyone is welcome to be heard.

3. Now that just about everything is online, group support is more widely available than ever. What I love most about online groups is that they offer you the chance to receive support and to offer support as well. You have a lot to offer others. One reliable way to shift a down mood is to be helpful and in service for someone else. While you're looking to receive support, you may find giving is also beneficial.

Social Media Groups

Unlike support groups, these connections tend to be more tenuous. There is still a lot of benefit here, not just in groups, but in posting from your own account. Groups can be very specific to a particular need or interest, like "grief over sudden loss of a sibling" or "early Pokémon collectors." I'm a part of several groups on topics like spirituality, mental health, and energy healing. Every day, people post prayer requests or ask advice for a problem. Almost always, group members respond with kindness and resources.

Someone I know recently posted, "Goodbye everyone!" on Facebook. This set alarm bells off within her friend group. One friend called the police, and they arrived at her home to perform a welfare check. Others started blowing up her phone with texts and voicemails. She had meant to put "Goodbye Facebook," since she was just planning a break, not to hurt herself! In the end, she was completely okay. At the same time, it was so heartwarming to see the outpouring of love and concern in the comments section. If it had been an emergency, a tragedy could have been prevented. I know social media generates a lot of aptly deserved cricism. At the same time, it's important to recognize how it can create connection.

See also the chapter "Finding Your People."

TIREDNESS

Our sweet bodies are getting zapped from too much stimulation. It's disrupting sleep and healthy digestions, making everyone overwired and overtired. This compromises immunity and makes you cranky!

Recognizing the amount of energy you have daily and managing it wisely is an act of self-compassion. Identifying when you're tired and choosing to give yourself rest, rather than chugging a heavily caffeinated beverage, or staying up for another two hours, is self-love at its most primal.

Getting Clear on Tiredness

1. What does it feel like in your body when you're tired? (e.g., tight neck, slumped shoulders, queasy stomach, sleepy, droopy eyes, headache)

2. What are some other signs of being tired you may have missed in the past? (e.g., getting irritable, feeling depressed, overreacting)

3. What depletes your energy? Who depletes your energy?

4. What increases your energy? Who expands your energy?

5. Remember the last time you felt truly rested. What circumstances were going on in your life at the time? Can you create that now? If so, how?

Make a commitment to consult your body on your activities and schedule. Our minds often think we are far more capable of endless stimulations while the body knows otherwise. If your body says NO, honor that.

Schedule downtime. Put it in the calendar to send a message to your subconscious that this is just as important as all your other tasks and responsibilities. Honor this time as you would any commitment.

> "We have to dare to be ourselves, however frightening or
> strange that self may prove to be."
>
> —MAY SARTON

2. Bridging the Inner Child and Yourself

When it's difficult to feel compassion for yourself, there's some inner-child healing that needs to happen. If, when we were small, we were shamed, blamed, or humiliated, a piece or pieces of our energy can be frozen in that time period. It's an important defense mechanism for the subconscious to shut down what we are unable to handle at the time it's occurring. It becomes problematic when those pieces remain cut off from our wholeness long after the original threat is gone. Those stuck pieces hold precious gifts for us to retrieve. And the best side effect ever? We have a greater capacity to hold compassion for all our parts, including the present-day version of ourselves.

Inner Healing Exercises

1. Journal with the Inner Child

   Hold an intention to connect with a child part who is ready to be home. Write: *Dearest inner child, I want us to be together. Where can I find you?*

Let the child answer and write through you. The location will likely be a metaphor, like at the bottom of a well or inside a corn maze. Other real-world possibilities are your childhood bedroom or grandmother's house.

Once you have a location, write: *How old are you?* (If you don't already know.) Let this come through and onto the page. If you don't get an answer, it may be a baby or toddler part.

Then write, *What happened?* Prepare yourself for whatever may come through and don't push for details that the child part isn't ready or even able to share. Be in a space of allowing.

Next write, *What do you need?* The answer may come in pictures or feelings rather than words.

Turn your awareness to your breath. Focus on the flow of air moving into and out of the lungs. Then begin imagining you are breathing in and out through the center of the chest. Do this until you feel a sense of warmth or calm.

Affirm to yourself, either silently or out loud: "I open the doors of compassion within my heart."

Feel that compassion energy grow, for that little person within you.

See this little part of you before you and create a bridge or cord between the child's heart and yours. See the energy of compassion moving through the cord to fill them up. Watch as they transform before your eyes.

Open your eyes and write again: *What do you need right now?* It might be the same answer as before or different. Whatever the response, do everything in your power to meet that need. Unless they ask for a pony. You'll have to do some explaining on that!

Close your eyes and return to the two of you and the bridge. Move closer, one step at time, until you are chest to chest and wrap them in a loving embrace. Tell them they are safe and dearly loved. Feel the energy of compassion moving within and between the two of you.

Melt your inner child into your arms so that two become one.

When you're ready, open your eyes and journal about this experience, making note of what compassion feels like.

2. Write Love Letters to Your Little Person

> *Start a daily practice of writing love letters to this little person within. What did you wish you were told as a child? How can you make them feel respected, loved, and valued? An example:*

Dearest Sweet Baby Boy Teddy,

I've been thinking about you all day. You are the best, most beautiful baby in the whole world! Your smile lights up my heart every time I see it. I want you to know, I do see you. And I love you so much. I'm so happy you are a part of me.

Love, Big Theodore

3. Lighting Up!

Every baby needs a person who lights up when they're seen. This is an important part of early childhood development. For many reasons, including logistical, not all of us received this. We are going to give this to ourselves now.

Close your eyes and imagine you are holding a sleeping baby version of yourself. If you have a baby picture of yourself, look at it and recreate this in your mind's eye.

See this baby open their eyes and begin to stretch.

Speak sweetness and adoration to them: "Oh, little darling, good morning! I'm so happy to see you, sunshine. How's my precious baby doing? Good? I bet! I'm so blessed to have you."

Image giving kisses and tickles. See yourself wrapping them in a snuggly blanket.

See the baby's eyes light up as they smile, giggle, and coo.

Whenever you are hard on yourself, return to this exercise. Feel the love, tenderness, and compassion move through your body. This can truly halt all the negative self-talk.

4. Use the 4–7–8 Breathing Technique

Healing can bring up anxiety because you're changing. Use this simple technique to calm the anxiety response.

Close your eyes. Breathe in through the nose to a count of 4. Hold for a count of 7. Exhale slowly through the mouth for a count of 8. Repeat five to ten times.

"Be yourself. Everyone else is already taken."

—OSCAR WILDE

QUICK BIT M2T LIST: THE POWER OF LANGUAGE #2

If you're partial to one or more of the adverse terms (e.g., Misfit, Geek) in the "Quick Bit M2T List: The Power of Language #1" on pages 59–60, you don't have to toss them aside. It's just time to reimagine, redefine, and reclaim them. This is something folks outside the status quo have always done. Now it's your turn!

Fill in the blanks with what the term means *to you.* I've included a few from my list and plenty of blank spaces to use for your own.

MISFIT
What I see when I say this:_____

What this means to me is:_____

Write and say: "I am reclaiming the word Misfit now!"

LOSER
What I see when I say this:_____

What this means to me is:_____

Write and say: "I am reclaiming the word Loser now!"

GEEK

What I see when I say this:_____

What this means to me is:_____

Write and say: "I am reclaiming the word Loser now!"

YOUR OWN TERMS:

_____

What I see when I say this:_____

What this means to me is:_____

Write and say: "I am reclaiming the word _____ now!"

_____

What I see when I say this:_____

What this means to me is:_____

Write and say: "I am reclaiming the word _____ now!"

_____

What I see when I say this:_____

What this means to me is:_____

Write and say: "I am reclaiming the word _____ now!"

_____

What I see when I say this:_____

What this means to me is:_____

Write and say: "I am reclaiming the word _____ now!"

6

Reclaiming Your Power

**"I FELT FREE, ONCE I REALIZED
I WAS NEVER GOING TO FIT THE
NARROW MOLD THAT SOCIETY
WANTED ME TO FIT IN."**

—ASHLEY GRAHAM

It's important to explore together how your natural power source of self-love was disrupted. I have found that this is very much part of the Misfit's journey. That perhaps no one can be born into a family, town, country, and time without being subjected to conditioning. If we didn't experience it, society could not function. There are agreed-upon rules for group conduct. Many of these are both necessary and innocent. When I pull into a parking lot, I'm going to park my car, as best as I am able to, between the two lines designating the space. If I parked sideways, taking up three spaces, not only am I taking much more room than needed, leaving fewer spots for others, I might have a heck of time getting my car out! So that's not what I'm talking about here. There's nothing radical or empowering about being thoughtless and inconsiderate.

The conditioning I'm going to explore here are the messages you received saying that you were not okay (for the many reasons people can dream up to assert that others are not okay). Much of this disempowering happened in childhood. But you may very well *still* be getting those messages. Please note all that apply.

Children are very susceptible to conditioning and forming beliefs. Especially about themselves. From birth until about the age of seven, a child's brain waves are mostly in theta and alpha states. These are the brain-wave states we experience during hypnosis and deep meditation. During those years, whatever children are exposed to goes right into the subconscious mind. Children have to rely on the information given from the people around them because their brains haven't yet developed the ability for rational thinking. So if when you were a baby, your mother repeatedly told everyone that she wished she'd had a boy instead of female you, this message would have been received by the subconscious. You could carry around a belief that you are defective in some way. Or wrong or bad. Or that all women are inferior. You may not have the memories of this to explain where these ideas came from.

> **"PEOPLE INSIDE OF BELONGING SYSTEMS ARE VERY THREATENED BY THOSE WHO ARE NOT WITHIN THAT GROUP. THEY ARE THREATENED BY ANYONE WHO HAS FOUND THEIR CITIZENSHIP IN PLACES THEY CANNOT CONTROL."**
>
> —RICHARD ROHR

THE BULLIED, SHAMED, EXCLUDED, OR ISOLATED INVENTORY

The following is a list of possible locations and relationships. I'm including these to help you identify times you felt shamed, bullied, excluded, or isolated. I've provided these options to prompt your memory. You'll have an opportunity to write about your experiences at the end of this chapter.

Locations

Home, school, church or other spiritual organizations, clubs / social organizations, college, including fraternities and sororities, internships, workplaces, online, out in public (stores, restaurants, etc.)

Relationships (Who)

Parents, stepparents, foster parents, grandparents, guardians, siblings, extended family and friends of the family, neighbors, friends, classmates, teachers, religious authorities (e.g., ministers, youth group leaders), club, class or group leaders (e.g., Girl or Boy Scout troop leaders, dance instructors), strangers (anyone you didn't know)

Once you've completed this, see if any of the following results resonate with you. Circle the ones that apply.

SOME RESULTS OF BEING BULLIED, SHAMED, EXCLUDED, OR ISOLATED

Make yourself small as to not draw attention to yourself

Quiet your voice (literally and figuratively), includes not disagreeing with others

Feel terrified of rejection so stay in relationships that aren't healthy

Try to get others' approval with what you look like, type of career, meeting the social standings of those around you (depends on region, culture, religion or not, income, educational standing), don't present your ideas (or let others take the credit for them), don't make waves (stand up for what you believe in), vacillate (you change to meet others where they are rather than being yourself)

EFFECTS OF LOW SELF-ESTEEM FROM BEING BULLIED

Eating disorders

Addictions (e.g., to phones, videogames, being right or wrong, people pleasing, attention—that is, addicted to praise and external validation, along with the more well-known addictions like alcohol, drugs, and food)

Under-achieving, under-earning

Relationship challenges

Do any of these effects resonate with you? Make a note in your journal and hold an intention to healing these.

> ## "I REALIZED THAT BULLYING NEVER HAS TO DO WITH YOU. IT'S THE BULLY WHO'S INSECURE."
>
> —SHAY MITCHELL

A Note on Professional Help

Each and every one of you is coming to this work with your own unique histories, ancestry, temperaments, support systems, and healing journeys and tools. If anything that follows in this chapter, the next, or any other part of the book feels too daunting, trust what your intuition and body are telling you. Get support. Support could be anything from free twelve-step groups like Codependents Anonymous to religious counseling in a community you're already a member of to professional services with an experienced trauma-informed coach, healer, or licensed mental health counselor. In my experience, self-guided healing is an important piece of getting empowered. After all, you are with yourself twenty-four hours a day. Only you can support and love yourself at the exact moment when it's needed, like if for example, as you leave a meeting in which you were humiliated. Only you will be there when an old memory pops up while showering. We go through so many triggers alone. It's imperative to learn how to nurture, support, love, and befriend (and/or mother) ourselves, not just in our true self-journey but in every journey for the rest of our lives. You have the answers within you. And there are times when outside support is exactly what is needed to get through the next hurdle, to hear those answers, to get that breakthrough. There is so much we don't know that no Google search can answer. In my own life I have a mentor, prayer partners, an energy-healer colleague I swap sessions with, a shaman, three body workers, and an ever-expanding list of healing friends from every background you can imagine (who I sometimes text at 11:00 P.M. with, "Got any tips for lower back pain?!? Can't sleep!"). Now consider my more normally employed friends of all ages who lend me support. They've literally experienced every possible circumstance life has to offer. Add an editor who occasionally needs to swoop in with wisdom, encouragement, and pep talks. (Are you exhausted just reading this? Think how I feel!) And if I needed it, I wouldn't hesitate to return to talk therapy as well. I've cultivated a cavalcade of places for support to aid me on my journey. Keep in mind, I do this work for a living. My spiritual and healer/healing journey is the central focus of my life. I can only go as far as my healing does. For me to come out of the shadows and rise in courage to convey this information so publicly, that support has been absolutely necessary. For you? Think both parts of your experience: your spiritual essence and your humanness. I speak to both aspects of us in my work because it's what works best. Getting both a prayer partner and a support group could be a great start.

If you've been abused, have experienced trauma in any way, feel disconnected or depressed and haven't yet sought professional mental health help, consider this to be an ideal time to do so. Rather than turn away from this material, it is possible that you picked up this book to accept an invitation from your Higher Self. An invitation to clear the old pain and programming. To become more of yourself. Maybe it is an invitation to fall in love with yourself too.

Reflection Questions

Take some time with these. We will be using the answers in the next chapter. You might start with jotting down some initial memories or insights, only to find others later coming to mind while driving, showering, or in dreams. Make a note of absolutely everything you can recall.

Let's start with intentions. Say out loud:

"My intention is to recall the most important times when I felt bullied, demeaned, shamed, and shunned. My intention is to recognize that today's date is _____ and I am now _____ years old. My intention is to only recall what is safe, right, and good for me to know. My intention is to recall this at the right time and in the right way. I declare it is safe to explore these memories to cleanse any old pain that may be inter-twined with them. Throughout this process, I am supported and guided by my Higher Self. (Feel free to affirm support and guidance from God, the Universe, Divine Mother, Allah, Jesus Christ, Archangel Michael, or any other deities: 'I am supported and guided by _____.') I am safe."

> **"OUR GREATEST GLORY IS NOT IN NEVER FAILING, BUT IN RISING UP EVERY TIME WE FAIL."**
>
> —RALPH WALDO EMERSON

When did you first realize that others thought you were different? How did you get this message? Were you called a name? Were you given "a look"? Were you treated differently?

When do you first remember feeling different from others? What was happening in your life at that time?

If you were ever bullied, list every time you experienced this. Take some time with this and let it flow over time.

QUICK BIT M2T LIST: EIGHT QUICK (AND FUN) WAYS TO REMEMBER WHO YOU ARE

1. Watch a movie with a Misfit to Trailblazer theme. See pages 169–170 to get you started on titles. Afterward, breathe into the inspirational feelings inside.

2. Put on music that celebrates uniqueness, self-love, and self-acceptance and DANCE! See pages 76–77 for song ideas.

3. Write a haiku to express your true essence. Originating in Japan, this type of poetry is known for its simplicity and brevity. Write three lines, with five syllables in the first, seven syllables in the second, and five syllables in the third. Don't overthink it! Just jot a few lines about who you are that not everyone sees.

4. Repeat affirmations that reveal your empowerment. A few general ones to get you started:

I am here on purpose.

I am remembering that my uniqueness is a gift to the world.

I am embracing all that I am now.

5. Write down three ways that life *is* working for you. Examples:

That promotion at work

My new friend Francois

That day last week when everything fell into place

6. Pick one thing you are always grateful for. Set a timer and spend three minutes imagining this in great detail, arousing the feelings of love and appreciation it inspires. Explain why you feel grateful for this.

Example: Your dog. Imagine them jumping up on the bed, licking your face, the softness of their fur, that special bark that says, "I'm ready to walk," how he looks when you wake up in the morning. Feel the love!

7. Doodle! Write your name in the center of your journal and doodle around it with lines, stars, smiley faces, hearts, spirals, or anything that shows movement from the center, radiating out in all directions.

8. Give yourself a hug. No, really! Wrap your arms tight around yourself and gently rock forward and back. This calms and soothes the nervous system.

7

Healing the Past

One of the great myths of emotional processing is this: time heals all wounds. Oh, how I wish this were so! That ignoring our emotional wounds would make them scab over and disappear. The truth? Time doesn't heal much. Yes, there are minor skirmishes and bumps we experience along the way in this thing called life. Those can and do simply slip away. But they are not the majority of what is plaguing us, particularly when we explore what's keeping us blocked from our best life. All of those times you were judged, labeled, excluded, and bullied have had a lasting impact. It is and will always be human nature to avoid pain. Hurting feels bad and we are innately inclined to bypass that. It's really just that simple. The impulse to run away from "bad" feelings is biological. Natural. That's why we all do it. And when that pain comes from a traumatic experience, avoidance is a lifesaving coping mechanism. Unfortunately, that coping mechanism outlives its usefulness in time. That avoidance leads to energy jams of unprocessed emotions in our precious bodies. They could be from an argument you had yesterday or one thirty years ago.

Imagine a shower drain. A single hair gets caught there. Summer comes and you start shedding like a golden retriever. Several more hairs congregate with the first. The water flow begins to slow. Even more hairs join the party. The water pools in the shower, eventually dripping down the drain. Then while rinsing your hair after coloring it, the drain becomes completely blocked. The water now stopped up in the shower, thickens and grows mold.

This is what happens in our emotional bodies.

I could have come up with a less disgusting metaphor here. But I use this one for a reason. I really want to get your attention. And who among us has never had a clogged sink, shower, or bathtub? It's a universal and utterly disgusting experience. When this happens, we will do whatever is necessary to clear that clog so the water drains. Ask me about the time I broke a beautiful jade chopstick shoving it into a clogged pipe.

I'd like you to approach processing your emotions with equal importance, with that same urgency. You don't want your emotional body to be the equivalent of a stinky, moldy, grime-packed tub.

All those unprocessed emotions are held in our energy field. Our energy field encompasses all parts of us, the ones we are easily aware of and the ones we aren't. Your physical body, appearing solid, is made of the same moving particles that encompass all of life. So when I say "energy field," don't leave the body out of this. I'm not speaking about some esoteric, invisible, hard-to-see spaciousness. I'm taking about all the levels and layers that make up the entirety of you. Unprocessed emotions trapped in the body have a tremendous negative impact on health and well-being.

SIGNS OF UNPROCESSED EMOTIONS

1. Lower physical energy or exhaustion

2. Nervous system dysregulation (high reactivity, shock, anger, and paralysis in circumstances that aren't life-threatening)

3. Depression
    Too much emotional suppression causes the entire body to feel suppressed. It feels exactly like depression and can be a key piece of this condition.

4. Anxiety
    A bundle of unprocessed anxiety leads to an expansion of it. For example, seemingly out of nowhere, you develop a fear of driving over bridges. You avoid bridges. Next, you notice your heart racing

on highways so you start taking back roads only. Finally, you get behind the wheel at home to start a drive. Before you can even back out of the driveway, the anxiety is unleashed, now leaving you unable to drive at all. Anxiety is letting you know you don't feel safe. Avoiding the emotional energy, by avoiding what appears to be causing it, increases the alarm bells going off.

5. ADD (attention deficit disorder) or ADHD (attention deficit hyperactivity disorder)
   Your focus shifts because you don't like feeling the way you currently do. This increases the more you suppress.

6. Addiction
   The world's most prevalent avoidance method. You have a bad day at work. Your colleagues invite you for happy hour. Two hours into half-priced drinks, you're no longer thinking about the humiliation you felt in the earlier meeting. But the energy of that situation still lives within you. Your lover dumps you for a new honey bunny. At the supermarket, your cart fills with ice cream and chips. At home, your food-fest pleasure binge momentarily masks the hurt. But that emotional pain still exists. Now factor in that substances like alcohol and sugar are highly physically addictive as well. It doesn't take much for an occasional outlet for relief to become a debilitating habit.

7. Poor memory
   Experiences you don't want to think about can lead to overall malfunctioning of your memory. Clients will often share with me that they don't have any childhood memories or any memories from an unhealthy marriage. All memories are stored in the subconscious mind; even after the conscious mind has forgotten or blocked them.

HOW TO PROCESS

1. Getting Honest

The first part of emotional processing is getting radically honest with yourself about how you feel. Feelings on their own are just an experience. Once our head gets involved in feelings, either we will deny because the truth is too painful or we will shame ourselves for having feelings.

Find a way of journaling that works for you. Not everyone resonates with writing thoughts and feelings down. Some choose to make recordings. Others will put their feelings into images. I've seen everything from squiggles and stick figures to magazine-clip collages and elaborate art. The point is to express. To find the perfect avenue for your feelings to be given a voice outside your head and body.

Once you've gotten honest, clear any blame you have for these feelings. Blaming your feelings can sound like "I'm blowing this out of proportion" or "Other people don't panic like this" or "I'm a bad (or weak or selfish or _____) person for feeling this way."

Judgments of our emotional experience shuts down all processing. Please know emotions will never, ever be logical. Allow whatever is there in the emotional body to be there.

AFFIRM:
I accept my feelings exactly as they are.
All feelings are welcome information.
I am a feeling being and I accept and allow every emotion.
Having feelings is an important part of being a human.
I am okay for feeling this way.

2. Cataloging Memories

Creating a time line can be a very helpful healing tool.

Turning a piece of paper in landscape position, draw a line three inches from the top, all the way from left to right. If you're over thirty, consider using a longer than standard sheet of paper. You'll need more room.

Put a marker at the beginning of the line that indicates birth. Put another on the right end that indicates the age you are right now. Put a series of dashes in between.

Start marking on the line major life transitions. Moves, various graduations, job beginnings and endings, relationship beginnings and endings. Then be sure to include any past painful experiences you can remember.

Pull the painful experiences out and create a separate list. As you glance at each one, put a checkmark next to the ones that make you feel cringey. Any discomfort is indicting a need for processing. Use the cringey memories for the next part.

3. Becoming Your Own Rescuer

You're going to go back in time and become the rescuer you needed then.

Close your eyes and begin to follow the trail of your breath.

Once you're relaxed, ask your subconscious mind to allow you access to that memory that happened at that time.

See it come into your mind's eye. Your subconscious may recall the memory literally, as it likely happened, or metaphorically, using imagery to symbolize the experience. Both are equally valid.

See this earlier version (EV) of you in need. Step into the image and let this EV know, "I am here to save you." Then do just that. Push the bully away. Tell your mom she's being mean. Put a cushion down to break EV's falls. Fix the situation. Then take EV's hand and bring them back to current time, letting them know they are safe and you will always be together.

Fitting In Versus Belonging

Fitting In

Imagine a jigsaw puzzle. All of the pieces are roughly the same size and shape with only slight variations. The colors and patterns have to be exact so they work together to create one image. Only the right and perfect piece will fit in the space it's designed for. Pull those pieces together, lock them into place, and you get the whole, complete, uniform picture.

Belonging

When I think of belonging, I see the ecosystem of a farm. There's the soil. That soil is filled with rocks, minerals, bugs, and water. Seeds are placed into the soil and then encouraged to burst open and move upward by rain and air. The sun incubates the force within the seeds, encouraging them to say yes to life. The farmer manages the soil and growing process, protecting the plants and encouraging the best results. This plot of land is surrounded by other plots filled with trees and other vegetation, all connected not only to this farm but to all that is. Birds fly overhead and drop their own unique fertilizer. Bees gather pollen and spread it around, allowing the crops to flourish.

Very few of the players in this scenario look remotely alike. The farmer doesn't look like the soil. The minerals in the soil don't resemble the sun. The seeds are completely unlike the rain. The birds and the bees have very different roles and abilities. But they comprise the thousands of parts that must come together in harmony for the plants that will eventually become food. Each being in their true essence, the players perform a natural symphony and absolutely everyone benefits. Every player benefits from living out its unique purpose and at the same time serves the greater whole. They belong with one another. And they belong to life and life belongs to them.

Can you imagine such a world? Can you see such a time? When each unique soul will be born into a family and community without pressure to conform. Little beings can learn about the voice of their inner compass, exploring all that their immediate surroundings have to offer. Each person has a soul, and much like a seed, there is a life force contained within it that is seeking to grow into what it is designed to be.

If we can create just such a world, I fully believe we will all experience the greatest sense of belonging any of us has ever known. It is the connection of owning our specialized part in the grand orchestra, the one that was designed for just us. As a result, our collective song of harmony, peace, love, and joy will grow and expand, *advancing each individual and the whole at the same time*. What music we will grow together!

The good news is we don't have to wait for everyone to get on board. In fact, they won't until we do. This is the M2T journey. We must start and start now. We came to show them the way.

We must grant ourselves the permission to break out of the past conditioning and listen for the call of our sweet inner song, beckoning us to our purpose, to our joy.

Our doing so helps everyone. Our doing so blesses the world.

M2T Journal Moment

1. *Write about a time in which you didn't fit in but you did belong.*

2. *Create an ecosystem and define your role within it. What does this environment look like? How are you contributing with your part? How are you benefiting from the contribution of the others around you, each inhabiting their perfect roles?*

8

There's More to Love

"FORTUNE FAVORS THE BOLD."

—LATIN PROVERB

In my late twenties I had had enough. I'd seen one too many movies and films where my momentary elation at an overweight character being introduced was quickly replaced with rage. These actors were morphed into roles playing dowdy, sad-sack wallflowers. Often the best friend of the gorgeous lead, these plus-sized characters would hopelessly whine about how no one could ever possibly want them because they're fat. Sniff. Pout. The stereotyping was absolutely ridiculous! The message from Hollywood was clear: "No one wants you ugly losers. Be grateful anyone who looks like you gets seen on screen at all."

Except, that wasn't the reality I or my other fabulously chubby friends were living. We had dates, boyfriends, and sex lives. We weren't sitting home on Saturday nights, stuffing our faces, sobbing, "Oh, woe is me." Each and every one of us was leading a dynamic, fascinating professional life and, yes, personal life too.

Who was pushing this nonsense? Why were people like us being stereotyped this way?

The plus-size fashion industry, then in its infancy, wasn't doing much better. My gorgeously curvaceous friend Leslie and I were elated to score tickets to a plus-sized fashion show in New York City. There it was, the catwalk, lit with spotlights, flanked by rows of chairs. It was an image we'd seen many times and now we'd be there in those seats, cheering on models who looked like us! Except, they didn't.

Not even close. The models were tall, like all models are. Except they weren't plus-size at all. Versus their size 2 counterparts who modeled for the superstar designers, these models were certainly larger, but none were bigger than an average size 10. They weren't actually plus-sized at all. If you had walked past them on the street, you would never consider them as large, heavy, overweight, or fat people. We felt completely defeated.

Soon after, I heard of auditions for a plus-size burlesque troop. I emailed the creator and told her I'd love to audition if I didn't have to do any nudity. She said they were looking for women who had the ability to dance well, make creative routines, and express sensuality, not vulgarity. I told her, "I'm your girl!" After my audition to the song "Fire Woman" by The Cult, I got one of the three coveted solo spots and adopted my dancing name: Ruby Whips. I wanted to use something sexy but also campy fun, like a drag name. Part of scoring this gig was spreading the word. After all, the whole idea of this had never been done before. We were expected to hit NYC nightclubs to find potential customers, a task I was more than happy to do. This ended up leading me to an opportunity I could never have expected.

Dancing at a downtown nightclub during Fleet Week, with about four too many tequila shots in my system, I was approached by two people on my way to the restroom. They said something about needing an actress for an independent movie. The details are blurry. I do know this. Forever the professional, I had handed them my ruby-red Ruby Whips business card. The man scribbled something on the back and handed it back over to me, which isn't what people do when you're giving them your contact information. I quickly went back to dancing into the night, without another thought.

The next morning I awoke with a hangover like no other. My mouth was carpeted with hay and I was so dizzy I had to hold the bathroom sink to stay upright. Normally not being much of a drinker, I wondered how to feel better fast. I grabbed my purse, looking for an Advil, when I pulled out my own card with a name, hotel, and phone number written on the back. It was only then I remembered the brief exchange from the night before, all of it shrouded in a haze. My intuition kicked in as I picked up the phone and dialed, uttering the name as

I was soon connected to a hotel room. I had no idea why I was calling or what I would even say. A rapid-talking British man answered and I stammered, "Uh, I met you last night and, um, you said to call, I think?"

"Oh, yes, great!" he said, and then proceeded to rattle off a hotel name and address. At some point I realized he was asking me to come back into the city to meet with them. Now. I had had about five hours of sleep, if passing out and sleep are the same thing, and I'm pretty sure they're not, but somehow I managed to shower, throw on a pair of velour cheetah-print pants and a black T-shirt, and drive into Manhattan. I remember arriving at the Lincoln Tunnel to zero traffic and gliding right through until I pulled up in front of a very chic hotel. It was only then that I realized whatever this was, it might actually be something.

The director Paul Lynch invited me up to his room, where he shoved a few pages of a movie script into my hands. "Go down to the lobby, and when you're ready to read, come back up." I was so hungover, I had to hold my head up as I sank into the large armchair in the lobby. I thought, *I'm not an actor! I've never acted in my life!* As I read through the dialogue, a conversation between two female friends, I didn't even know which one I was up for!

After about five minutes, I thought, "This is *never* going to happen. I'll just wing it and get this whole thing over with so I can tell people this great story about how I auditioned for a movie one time." (And look, I'm doing that right now!)

When I returned to the room, Paul and his assistant had me run through the lines. I was utterly awful. But instead of kicking me out, they kept me there for another two hours as they explained what this movie was all about. Titled *More to Love*, it was the story of an overweight woman who breaks out of her mundane life, makes a friend to show her the way (that would be my character), and finds love. They set up a camera and interviewed me about my experience as a large lady and what I thought about how women like me were depicted in movies and TV. All those criticisms I had been screaming at screens for years? Those insights finally had a place to be well received. Here was a person, a film director no less, who actually wanted to know what *I* thought. Paul was so respectful, curious, sensitive, and kind. I found myself easily opening up and sharing my experiences.

He genuinely wanted to know what life in a larger body was like. He casually mentioned the love interest for the lead would be played by none other than Maxwell Caulfield, my childhood crush, who had ridden into my heart like the second coming of James Dean in *Grease 2*. When I gasped, he asked, "Oh, you've heard of him?" The entire experience was so surreal. It was as if I woke up in an alternate universe. Auditioning for a movie? Providing input on a script? Being interviewed by a director? And Maxwell freaking Caulfield was involved? Maxwell. Freaking. Caulfield. How on earth was this happening?

I may have stumbled into this situation but I left sauntering, on a high with my head held high. Never thinking I'd get the part, I had hoped to be asked to be a consultant, that a place could be made for my experience and insights.

Then the producer called me. I got the part! I went into complete shock. I didn't know how to act! And what about my social service job I had been at for a little over a year? A new statewide initiative I had worked on was about to launch. How would I get the time off? Unfortunately, my CEO told me to take the time and go. I say "unfortunately" because I wanted her to say no so I'd have the perfect excuse to say, "No, sorry, can't do it." I told my bestie, Ulana, "I can't do this. I just have a bad feeling about this." It ends up that "bad feeling" wasn't a premonition. It was anxiety. Ulana said, "You need to do this. You need to go." Utterly terrified and completely broke, I exchanged my collection of 120 Susan B. Anthony one-dollar coins for bills and hopped a train, Canada-bound.

When I got there, I was brought to the production office. Right in the center was a huge piece of wood nailed to the wall, with rows of spaces marked with masking tape. Each square contained the character's name above the headshot of the actor playing them. Next to the lead actress, Louise, was a space labeled Fran, my character, and a big empty space glaring back at me. I didn't have a headshot. Because I wasn't an actor. And by the way, what the hell was I doing there?!

It was a moment I've relived in so many circumstances throughout my lifetime. One of these things is not like the other. And that thing is me!

Later I was approached by an actress who was an extra. She made sure to tell me that she had auditioned for my role and was so surprised they went with "an unknown." Unknown? How about nonexistent, lady!

Then I saw the director yelling at one of the actors playing a main character before we were even reintroduced. And I thought, "Uh-oh. What have I gotten myself into here." I don't think anyone enjoys being yelled at, but for highly sensitive people like me, it's devastating.

And just like that, within an hour, I got sick. High fever, stuffy nose, puffy eyes. Not exactly the look one is going for before their film debut. Even then, years before I would become a healer, I knew this was emotional. I had believed I didn't belong there. My body was making it easy for the powers that be to agree with me. It almost felt like a relief. I hadn't yet been on camera. They could just fire me and I could go back to my regular life, instead of trying to learn to act while being *in* a film.

But I wasn't getting off that easy.

They fed me cold medicine and fruit. The star's personal assistant, who essentially had nothing to do, was reassigned as my personal keeper. Every time I turned my head she was there with water, echinacea, and vitamin C.

And then the strangest thing happened. After my first few scenes, the director was pleased. No yelling. No insults. He *liked* what I was doing. I couldn't believe it! It allowed a courageous knowing to come forth from inside me. **I claimed my right to be there.** After all, they had auditioned hundreds and landed on me, a drunk dancing diva they saw in a club. There must be a reason for it. And within a day, the sickness was completely gone.

Later, when another actor implied I hadn't "paid my dues," I replied, "I may not have paid my acting dues, but I have sure as hell paid my life dues." If anyone deserved a break, it was me. And that was that. The bullying and gossip ended, and the rest of the experience was one of the highlights of my entire life. I was encouraged to suggest lines and some of my real-life experiences influenced the finished film. I was respected and valued. Plus, film-geek me got to experience just how movies are made while schmoozing with my movie-star crush on set.

Later, the movie went to a film festival and was briefly on TV, and yours truly got her fifteen minutes of fame. The courage it took to say yes once paid off in many magical ways over the next few years.

I learned so much from this, which I highlight below.

Pay Attention to When You're Fed Up

Fed up with how you're being treated or depicted. Fed up with an injustice. Fed up with a relationship or job. That feeling is speaking to you. It's letting you know it's time to take a stand for who you really are. It's time to say no to what isn't working so you can be open to what is. A breakthrough awaits on the other side of this courage.

Be Willing to Be a Voice for Others

In the movie, there were scenes that take place in a club with many full-figured extras. During the inevitable downtimes that come with movie-making, some of the extras shared how important this movie meant to them. They too had been tired of being stereotyped. This gave me a purpose and allowed me to speak up and be much more assertive than I had been previously capable of. Being a voice for others gives us access to courage and

> **"DON'T WORRY ABOUT NOT FITTING IN. THE THINGS THAT MAKE PEOPLE THINK YOU'RE WEIRD ARE WHAT MAKES YOU YOU, AND THEREFORE YOUR GREATEST STRENGTH."**
>
> —BIRGITTE HJORT SØRENSEN

power we normally wouldn't be able to access for ourselves. Be willing to be used for the greater good.

The Power of Detachment

In the two decades since my hotel-room audition, I've seen various actors interviewed who say they get the roles they're least attached to and never expect. I am not normally a "winging it" kind of person. I'm more a "get nervous, over prepare, try way too hard, and mess it up" kind of person. During the audition, my complete lack of experience combined with one mutha of a hangover led me to just give up and make it up as I went along. Remember, I wasn't even sure what I was doing there. And there was never a single moment when I thought I'd be cast.

I've been encouraged ever since to use the power of detachment to draw beautiful people and opportunities into my world. I understand it now in ways I didn't then. If I'm mentally grasping too tightly to what I want, the energy in that opportunity cannot flow, and it acts as a repellent rather than an attractor. When I can be light and easy about it all, trusting the outcome will be for my highest good and knowing there's always another miracle around the corner, I don't have to covet. I can let go and let it flow.

Claim Your Damn Space!

If you don't think you belong, you can be sure that will be reflected back to you in painful ways. Everyone deserves to be where they are; that's why they're there. It is easy for those outside a situation to judge another's worthiness. But the truth is, you have no idea about the whole story of a person, not even your partner. And you know even less about their soul's journey and how that journey fits into the wholeness of the Universe. Normally we judge when that person has what we want. If there was one spiritual truth I wish every single person knew, it would be this: there's more than enough good for every one of us. Inevitably when I say this, someone will chime in with, "What about all the starving people?" Here's a hard-to-hear truth. People are not starving because there's not enough food. There's more than enough food for everyone on the entire planet. Fifty percent of the food produced in the United States is thrown out! That ugly tomato and dented can? They end up in a landfill, along with all the expired chicken. So it's not that there's not enough, there are problems getting it to the people who most need it, another issue entirely. Another person will chime in with, "But all the good ones are taken." I reply, "You're a good one and you're not yet 'taken.'" For every doubt you have about this, there is someone, right now, who is getting that wonderful job or marrying that incredible person. It can be you too. For abundance, all we need do is look to nature. Any farmer will tell you that plants produce way more seeds than can ever be planted. The earth is abundant. Opportunities are abundant. Boldly claim your space in your family, school, workplace, hobby group, or community. Start by doing this internally. Affirm you are worthy of being seen, heard, and valued. See yourself in a chair at the "movers and shakers" meeting. Or leading a discussion in the moms' group or PTA. Practice it in your mind. Arouse the feelings of being exactly where you want to be. Then take your freaking place! Step in and do it. Do it even if your knees are shaking. Do it even if you feel like you will spontaneously combust. It will get easier with time, but you can't wait to feel 100 percent calm before you make a move. You'll never be completely without fear when making a positive change. Claim your space now!

That person who has what you don't believe they deserve? *They* believe they deserve it. They don't care that they don't have the degree or started at the company four years after you. They're not waking up in the middle of the night, gripped with guilt at their good fortune. No, they claimed their space and then inhabited it like they had been born there. Those supposedly undeserving people can be role models. Not for any unethical, illegal, fraudulent behavior. That's not at all what I'm talking about. In fact, mimicking those behaviors will certainly get you in trouble with the Universe, and also likely the law. You don't have to like them. They may, in fact, not be what we consider "good people." But they are living examples of what you need to learn. You can study their movements and language. Let them show you what claiming looks and sounds like.

What Feels Like "Something Bad" May Be Anxiety

When a client tells me, "I just know if I do this, something bad will happen," I know we are dealing with anxiety. Especially so if they follow this with, "And I know it's not my anxiety." Premonitions and other intuitive nudges don't sound like panic. Their feeling tone is neutral. In fact, you can receive intuitive nudges in the body, without your mind knowing what's happening at all. I remember walking in a park on a sweet, sunny day, when I was suddenly filled with strong foreboding in my body. I was in a great mood and my mind could not understand why I was feeling this way. But I've learned to stop, listen, and trust. This feeling was unmistakable. Something, I had no clue what, was wrong. Even though I had two laps to go, I jumped in my car and left. As I was driving home, out of nowhere, hunks of hail the size of golf balls began to bounce off my hood, followed by pounding rain and severe winds. I got home just before it intensified. A tornado no one had expected ripped through my town! The next day, the park was filled with downed trees, including several that fell across the very path I had been walking on. My intuition was working well that day!

Anxiety, on the other hand, can easily be aroused whenever we are moving out of our comfort zone. If you're facing an opportunity or pursuing a goal, that "bad feeling" is just trying to hold you back in the safe zone. Learn to recognize the signs of anxiety in the body. Stomach in knots; tightness in the chest; sweaty hands, head, and feet; shoulders rising up to the ears; and a jumpy leg are classic signs to look out for. Once you're aware of what it is, you'll be more empowered to calm that response in your body before it sabotages something that could be very, very good for you.

Most of us Misfits experience anxiety. After all, there are times we've been targeted or shunned. Our nervous systems become very jumpy and overactive in order to keep us safe. Hypervigilant. Learning how to calm and regulate your nervous system will become an essential life tool.

QUICK BIT M2T LIST: FOUR DAILY PRACTICES TO SUPPORT YOUR M2T TRANSFORMATION

1. Prayer

You are more than just a body and a brain. You are an infinite spiritual soul, here for a purpose. Connect with the Universe either by asking for or affirming guidance, support, and timely revealing of what you're here to do.

Examples:

> Dear Universe, who am I really and how do I best serve today?

> Universe, please show me who I am and lead me to the right people, places, and experiences today that enliven my journey.

> I am one with an all-knowing, all-powerful Universe and I am shown the magnificence of my true being today. I am guided to my rightful place.

2. Loving Your Physical Form

Take a moment to think of something or someone you truly love. Now take that expansive energy and send it to every part of your body, face, and/or hair. Love the skin you're in!

3. Processing Your Feelings

Journal for a few minutes when you get up in the morning. If anything pokes the Misfit wound during your day—like a snarky comment—make time to visit those feelings in the evening. Uncensor yourself and confront the offender on paper until you feel lighter. (Do not send it to the person! It's for your eyes only.)

Take time to close your eyes and feel the sensations in your body that are holding uncomfortable emotional energy. Gently witness them while you imagine breathing in and out of these areas. If the intensity lessens, you are allowing the emotions to move.

4. Imagining Your Empowered Self

Close your eyes and see yourself being your true self and loving your life. See supportive, loving, good people embracing you. Feel the power as you see yourself realizing your goals.

Just start with this. Your imaginings will change and morph over time.

"TO BE BEAUTIFUL MEANS TO BE YOURSELF. YOU DON'T NEED TO BE ACCEPTED BY OTHERS. YOU NEED TO ACCEPT YOURSELF."

—THICH NHAT HANH

9

Revenge

**"DON'T SEEK REVENGE. INSTEAD,
BECOMES SO GOOD THAT YOU SIMPLY
MAKE THEM REGRET."**

—MARK MANSON

My greatest accomplishments have been motivated by revenge, and other confessions on a spiritual path. (I'm convinced this will be the title of my autobiography.)

You will be underestimated.

That same energy that lets others know you're different will lead them to believe major fallacies about you. That you're weak. Untalented. Unacceptable. Unlistenable. Unwanted.

And you're going to use that to prove them wrong.

You will be thwarted.

Then there are the bullies and blockers, the betrayers and shamers. Those that don't want you to flourish in your power. Because, after all, how can they inflate themselves unless you're underneath them?

This is where revenge becomes your best friend.

Who among us hasn't harbored a secret revenge fantasy? It's inspired by the mistreatment or ignorance of others for a good reason. It's the theme of thousands of plots, probably since storytelling began. It's a pivotal aspect of human behavior and it can be your greatest motivator.

Many people, particularly spiritual people, will tell you that your revenge feelings are wrong. That those feelings are destructive and will boomerang bad mojo back on you. That they will leave you with regret and bitterness. And to that I say, not if you use revenge in the right way.

To be clear, I am not suggesting you mass text revenge porn or burn a house to the ground. I'm not even hinting that you should spread malicious gossip or trash-talk the people who have hurt you. **Clearly hear me on this.** No revenge that is damaging to others! I would never encourage any harmful or violent behavior in any way. Not only would this add to the ever-growing toxicity of a conflict-ridden world, it will harm people. Not just the person you want to harm. These acts will harm you and unsuspecting bystanders. It's both globally and personally devastating.

I'm going to share with you one of my most shameful acts.

When I was fifteen, after my parents moved from a New Jersey suburb to the Tampa area of Florida and I was struggling to find my way, an unexpected angel popped into my life. I'll call her Jane. She was blond, stunningly beautiful, with crystal-blue eyes and clearly not a weirdo like me. I had no idea where she came from or why she was even talking to me. Suspicious, I remained reserved. But I just couldn't shake her. She sought me out over and over again, and I finally gave in. Here was what I had needed so badly. A new friend! Soon we were talking on the phone every night and hanging out after school, and I'd gladly tag along when invited to her gig as a dance class assistant. Jane was the first of many X-factor friends I would come across throughout my life. All of them were conventionally beautiful, charming, incredibly charismatic, and beloved. They oozed the megawatt attractor factor but were somehow incomplete without a smart and sassy sidekick, who could never compare in the looks department. Enter me, the proverbial helpful and supportive "bridesmaid," uplifting behind the scenes to support the far more alluring and glamorous "bride." I got something out of these scenerios too. It was a way of being close to power but never actually stepping into my own. As long as I didn't believe in my own beauty, my own charisma, it was projected onto this series of friends. With them, I was wanted and valued, as long as I remained a "best supporting" and didn't try to step into the "lead." In other words, I *had* a place as long as I *stayed* in my place. As a Misfit, being in the shadows was comfortable for me. After all, everyone told me that my very existence was unacceptable. Once that was ingrained, no one else needed to put me at the bottom of the list. I did it all myself.

As inexplicably as Jane befriended me, I was unceremoniously dropped without any signs or warnings. One day I approached her in a school hallway and she semipolitely blew me off. Phone calls were not returned. Excuses were made. Until I finally got it. I had been dismissed, leaving me completely befuddled and deeply crushed. I didn't realize at the time that she had hit on my core wound of rejection. I searched through all of our shared memories. Did I say or do something wrong? Did my tormentors get to her, convincing her I was a freak? Why did she do this? There were no answers. It didn't take long for my hurt to boil into blind rage.

Fortunately, I had made some other, steadier, big-hearted friends in the meantime. All of them unique, fascinating, and genuine worshippers at the altar of punk rock. In other words, just my style! You may remember from my earlier mentioning of Stephanie, Mike, Chris, and Lou. We were settling into quite a crew due to my relentless recruitment practices. I was always scanning the hallways like a hawk, looking for anyone the least bit off. Is that a Cure button on that vest? Do I spot a vintage rhinestone bracelet over there? I still cringe a bit when I remember how in my own awkward way, I'd say, "Hey, join us. There's safety in numbers. You've got safe spaces here. You've got new friends here. We will understand you." I was determined. Not everyone accepted my invite, but Stephanie definitely did. It's interesting because, like Jane, Stephanie was also very blond and very beautiful, oozing with charisma and that magical X-factor appeal. At the same time, she was (and still is) genuine, grounded, trustworthy, incredibly kind, generous, and loyal. Her intelligence and wit made for interesting and hilarious conversations, the kind I couldn't have with Jane. I can see it so clearly now, all these years later. Miraculously, a void had been filled with a far better friend, someone I still dearly love all these decades later.

That should have been enough. But it wasn't. I couldn't see then how the Universe was acting in my life. Ruminating in my head, I couldn't shake what Jane had done to me. The injustice! The cruelty! I would make her pay!

Like someone running for political office, I rallied my friends to come around to my way of thinking. I provided compelling evidence of what I thought was Jane's obvious evilness. A couple of my peeps had had their own fleeting brushes with her as well, so it wasn't a hard sell. I had made her the enemy and wanted company in this. She was a bad person and must be informed of this. In my bitter brewing, I did something horrible.

I was out shopping with a friend when we came across a greeting card. On the cover it said, "With friends like you . . ." and on the inside it said, ". . . who needs enemies" with a cartoon of a person being stabbed in the back. We bought it, and a few of us wrote terrible things to Jane in it. I was filled with an unsettling anxiety that I confused for righteous excitement. I don't remember how we got the card to her, but I did hear back that she had been absolutely devastated by it. But before I even learned of her reaction, I had already been carrying a sinking, sickening guilt. Oh my God, what had I done? I briefly attempted to double down and assure myself she deserved to be punished. Wasn't this just retribution for what *she* had done? Hadn't she in some way brought this on *herself*? I fought to justify it. First to myself. Then to others.

But I knew. I had become what I most hated. Now I was the bully. Now I was cruel. Wrong is wrong. And it made me sick.

The sweet celebration of revenge, of comeuppance, was nowhere to be found. I felt uglier than I ever had before because now I knew there was ugliness inside of me. Whatever power or closure I thought it would bring me, it had just deepened the wound. I may not have liked the way she treated me, but now I didn't like myself very much either. It didn't fix or heal anything. I tried to avoid thinking about it, filled with nervous, jumpy energy, but night after night, there it was, the shameful act I could never undo, keeping me wide awake. When you tread lightly on the earth, feeling deep sensitivity, treating others as you'd like to be treated, staying in touch with profound compassion for all suffering, the very nature of guilt is a foreign, chaotic, dizzying experience. I didn't know what to do with it. Anxiety, check. Anger, check. Depression, check. They were all so familiar at that point and I was doing my very best to manage them. But this?! I wondered how cruelty could exist in any form. How is it that there are people with no conscience? How do they do it, continually hurting others? How do they live with themselves? I was clearly not built for bullying.

It was a very powerful lesson for me that I'm glad I got at such an early age. There will be people in life who treat you poorly. Especially if you don't fit in. And feelings of wanting to exact revenge can be a natural side effect of that treatment. But retaliation will make you feel far worse, not better. And feeding that energy creates a ripple effect going out into the ethers, wreaking havoc on people and situations you'd never expect, including yourself. Confucius said, "Before you embark on a journey of revenge, first dig two graves." He got it, clearly understanding the nature of that energy. Whatever feelings you feed perpetuates an ever-growing cycle of them. And there are countless examples of misplaced pain leading to revenge violence, like horrific mass shootings at schools. I knew, I didn't want to feed the pain, trauma, and outrage of a world already out of balance. I don't ever want my hurt to hurt anyone else. I'm here to help, not hurt. I'm here to love, not shun. I'm here to help restore the balance, not tip the scales. And that is true for you too.

So this left me with quite the conundrum. I have a natural urge for vengeance. It feels almost biological in nature. Maybe it's because I'm half Italian. There is a stereotype for vendettas for people of my heritage, though that's clearly not the case for most Italians. But I'm still going to partially blame it on my blood. That's the primal, nature part. Then there's lots of experiences of trauma and bullying. That's the nurture part. And along with this urge, I have possessed an erratic tendency to occasionally *still* attract the most deplorable behavior of others. People who have suppressed their creative power often do. Check out the description of the Crazy Makers from Julia Cameron's classic creative-block-busting book *The Artist's Way*. You can find the description online, but I also highly recommend reading the book and following her program as outlined. You may recognize your unpleasable boss or your dramatic, self-absorbed friend. Crazy Makers are poking you to express your own creative urges. And here's the thing, once you *do* embody your creative powers, you will attract people who feel threatened by them. It certainly doesn't *have* to be this way, but it often is. It's difficult to even express how sad this makes me. Rather than allowing you to be an ally, a helper, or just a real-life example of a person who gives themselves permission to share their unique gifts, you can become an enemy, having done nothing harmful to them at all. If the way people treat you is getting you down, revenge fantasies can be a natural side effect.

What's a conscious, kind, and ethical person to do?

This brings me to the next most famous quote on revenge: "Living well is the best revenge," an uplifting message from George Herbert, a seventeenth-century poet.

Now *this* was something I could get behind. And that's exactly what I did and still do.

I do it each time my good-natured earnestness is met with betrayal. Every time the whispers of deception find their way to my ears. Each time a commitment is broken, without any acknowledgment or apology. All the situations where others use my work in their own without crediting me. Or even asking. Or quoting me without acknowledgment. Very easy to happen in the times we are living in. Those circumstances can become my most powerful motivators.

Never underestimate the power of: I'll show them!

Turn the situation around! When you think of all the bullies, the suppressors, the power-hungry Hungry Hippos chomping down on you, reframe their actions as an invitation for you to grow. To show up for yourself. To push yourself forward in ways you've been telling yourself you can't. To explore more of what you have to offer. To surprise yourself. To move you out onto your growing edge. To rise up.

I'll share a few examples from my life.

A few years ago, I was a newly, fully self-employed healer after six years of doing this work part-time along with my full-time jobs. To work for myself and grow my practice was an immediate relief. Now I could devote my entire life to what my soul came here to do. It was also completely terrifying! This was sink-or-swim time, and my sea legs were shaky. Creating 100 percent of my income was now completely up to me. There were no safety nets. No surplus of savings. No side hustles. No other source of income. I was completely confident in my ability to serve my clients. I had fifteen years of traditional counseling experience and business skills from my nonprofit years. I had spent several thousands of hours, over decades, taking classes, studying, and practicing my skill set. And the clients that I had worked with clearly benefited. I knew that I'm really good at this. My devotion to the work and these practices was paying off. But would this translate into a full-time, self-sustaining career? Could I earn what I had been making or even more? Just because I was an effective healer didn't mean I could create a successful business. If you ever take a look around for failed business stories, you'll soon be toppling over them. And when you doubt yourself, you'll find even more examples of failure! I was given a thousand reasons to just get another job. Another steady paycheck. The road more traveled. Which would have made for an easier life, just not the rich kind of life I really wanted to be living. I was risking it all and desperately in need of support, encouragement, and mentoring.

In this vulnerable state, still stinging from having been fired from my last job, I traveled out of town for a big speaking and teaching gig. The pressure was building within me. Could I show up and shine? Would this lead to more visibility and thus more clients? Would I make enough money to cover my travel costs, at the very least? Each night my sleep was rocked by anxieties.

I arrived in town for the event feeling like a lost little girl, eager to please and be accepted, while wearing a mask of happy confidence. I was happily surprised to be invited to a few social events with new-to-me colleagues. I was so excited to be included. All of these professionals were far more experienced and well known in the field than I was. All of them had successful practices I had long admired and aspired to. This was my chance to get to know them and maybe even to interview them a bit, to hear their success story. I wanted to find out how they developed their businesses, what the secrets were to their success, and what it's like to do this work full time. In my nervousness and feeling like an outsider, I shut down and

I didn't say much, trying to get a feel for everyone and follow the conversations. After all, they all knew one another well and I didn't know any of them. When I finally did say something, I made one ridiculous comment after another, spilling out of my mouth like an unstoppable waterfall. I made all the wrong moves. What had happened to any semblance of intelligence or wit? They had clearly vacated my brain, leaving me tongue-tied, stammering, and cringing. I had tried way too hard and failed miserably.

That's my part in all this. And then there were the reactions from the people present. The callousness and rejection I received from a couple of those people left me in complete shock. There were mean comments and looks of disgust. I was treated as an unwelcome presence, an interloper, a total embarrassment, even though I had been invited. This was neither subtle nor in my imagination. In every way it could be made known, where I had initially been included, I was now being sharply elbowed out. It was clear, I hadn't made the grade. One of the people even insulted me in front of others, and I could tell the others were visibly confused and uncomfortable. They were embarrassed for me. All of it absolutely leveled me. I had been so vulnerable, so unsure of myself, so needing acceptance from—let's face it—this group of other Misfits. Healers of all kinds are misunderstood at the least, ridiculed at the worst. And after all, don't we *help* people who have anxiety, who've been bullied, who are starting businesses and are letting go of who they've been told they are to become their true selves? I had hoped for a tender welcoming into the fold. Instead, I felt humiliated and absolutely crushed. An event that I had hoped, and prayed, would go so well could not have been worse. Why, Universe, why??? I spent so much time sobbing in a hotel room that I looked like I had been repeatedly punched, all red-faced and puffy-eyed.

And that's when my old friend Revenge came a-calling, to pull me out of my pitying despair and give me a much-needed kick in the ass.

But this Revenge wasn't the maniacal, out-of-control, petty rage machine of my youth. I'm sure you've met that version out in public before. You may have seen her artistry in the spray-painted CHEATER on a car's door. Or listened to her tale of betrayal on a podcast or social media, complete with the naming of names.

Or read one of her Yelp reviews, where she assails with searing insults, perhaps without sharing much factual information to back up her complaint.

No, not at all. This Revenge was a brand-new kind of cat. How unsettling! First off, this Revenge was not a yeller. She'd never give you the satisfaction of seeing her out of control. She showed up cool, calm, and cunningly calculating. It didn't take long for her to push the whimpering little girl inside me aside and completely take over. "Fuck them," she said, "we're going to be better and do better than any of them could have ever imagined. They've underestimated you. That gives you the power now. This isn't new. Now is the time for you to show them who you truly are." And that was it.

She picked me up and dried my face. Then she drew the deepest, darkest, and sharpest eyeliner across my lids and painted the rubiest red across my lips. Then she said, "Oh yes, there they are," to those eyebrows that say, "Better back the fuck up." My version of war paint, my makeup tells a story. This story was, "Guess what? I'm in charge now."

I pulled out the notes for my talk and gutted them, new ideas flooding through me as I captured every single one. I let go of what I should talk about and decided to say exactly what I wanted. Any need to be liked and accepted was gone, baby, gone. This Revenge said, "Time to burn the boats." In other words, there would be no going backward. This freedom, where you don't have the need for approval and will proceed as you choose, it's like its own unique form of ecstasy! And I had my "buddies" to thank for it. My Spirit and the Universe boosted my energy level, dropping inspiration after inspiration and cheering me on! I guess I hadn't been abandoned after all. Not by what and who matters most. Talk about turning a situation around!

When it came time for me to speak, I bounded onto the stage with confidence and grace. Speaking with absolute authority and genuine power, within seconds I knew the audience was with me, full attention on every word. Not a mask or a performance, there was no reality-show fake bravado here. My true essence emerged, and I was simultaneously informing, entertaining, inspiring, moving, *and* downright funny! It was intoxicating! I suddenly realized why stand-up comedians do what they do. I knew immediately that the audience and I were falling in love with one another. We were all together and we were all in. If every time I had metaphorically dropped the mic I had physically dropped it, I'd still be paying for the replacements today. My speech ended with great enthusiasm and cheer. I did it!

The strangest experience happened just as I was leaving the stage, utterly triumphant in every way. My gaze somehow landed on that person I had felt the most hurt by. To my surprise, all I felt for them was pure, overflowing love. The resentment or anger had completely vanished, along with my judgments. I had fallen in love with every person in that room, including them. They may have excluded me, but my love was so big, it included them. My love is just that generous. It's just that enveloping. My power met the Universe's power, and it was just that enormous, that all-encompassing, that unifying that there was room for all, and I wouldn't have wanted it any other way.

They had helped me bring the best of myself, my true self, out onto the stage that day. They helped me release the need to be liked. It hadn't worked anyway! They ended up being an integral part of my very success. My mind was blown! They hadn't held me back or undermined me. Why? *Because I didn't let them.* They had lifted me up! I could never have imagined this was even possible when I was crying on my bed not so many hours before. But this Revenge, she knew. She knew I needed to delve deeply into myself and unearth my divine powers, to show them who I am. I let her take me further than the rest of me knew I could go.

This Revenge packed her suitcase and sunk back into my depths, beaming from a job well done. She's always on the ready to return when I most need to get moving forward. (I think I saw a pair of red stiletto heels in there.)

A note: I can't know this for sure, but I suspect if I had felt emotionally safe enough to be my true self with my colleagues, circumstances could have unfolded differently from the very start. Awkwardness and desperation to be liked are always repellents. It gives others an icky feeling in your presence. After all, the true me is a fascinating person. An interesting and thoughtful person. And, generally, a good conversationalist, as I very much enjoy asking people about themselves, their views, and their worlds. My healing work starts with finding out what makes my clients tick and uncovering what created the struggles they are seeing me about. I have a bit of a detective in me. People tend to like the people who take a sincere interest in them. And I've never met a boring person yet. Because of my own insecurities at that time, my colleagues were repelled and missed out on the real me. And I missed out on them. If only I could have felt secure. More confident. Perhaps I would have been treated more kindly, more respectfully. But the truth is, I didn't feel safe. I didn't feel safe with where I was in my career. I didn't feel safe being myself. Not in that instance. And I didn't feel safe with them. May we all manifest a community of people we feel safest with.

The moral of this story? Take the doubters and the haters, the hurters and betrayers, and let them motivate you.

Create your happiest, healthiest, most successful, unique, beautiful life. Take the focus off of them, their criticisms, their repugnant behavior. They wouldn't act that way if they loved themselves and their lives. The saying is true: hurt people hurt people. Loving people love people. Including themselves. Be an example of self-love by loving yourself into your best life. Then your next best life. Then the one after that. Because life never stays the same and neither will you.

Then you may be able to find the motivation to forgive them. Find compassion for what they must have gone through to become that mean. And consider that what you perceived as cruelty may just have been cluelessness on their part. Every experience we see through the filter of our own limited perception. See the wider picture, invite a more enlightened perspective, generously share your mercy. In fact, this likely will happen. After all, when your needs are met, your goals are being realized, and you have the love and acceptance you've been craving, bestowing forgiveness and mercy is easy to do.

M2T Journal Moment

1. *Describe a time when you were hurt or betrayed. Who was involved? What happened? How did you feel and how did you behave?*

2. *Rewrite the script. Take the same exact scenario from question 1, with the same person or people. Then rewrite the final part. Access your Empowered Revenge. Write how you would have liked to feel and liked to have responded.*

3. *Describe your Empowered Revenge avatar. What do they look like, sound like, and wear? (Example: a six-foot-four Adele clone in a lemon-yellow vinyl bodysuit, commanding in a booming voice, "Let's go!") Use your imagination and have fun with this.*

QUICK BIT M2T LIST: THREE COURAGEOUS ACTS TO PRACTICE

Courage is a quality to be practiced and strengthened, just like a muscle. One or more of these can help you face your fears. After, you'll realize you didn't spontaneously combust after all. Do them enough until they feel easy.

1. Wear a ridiculous or even bizarre outfit. Wrap yourself in colored duct tape. Clip a plastic bird in your hair. Paint one side of your face. And no, not on Halloween! Do your regular errands. Act as if everything is perfectly normal, like you have no idea that anything about you is amiss. Don your best poker face. Ignore any stares or comments. Later, laugh about it with a friend. Or ask a friend to tag along behind you, recording some of the reactions!

2. Do some public speaking. Sign up for an open-mic night. I don't care if you're not a writer or musician. Read your grocery list! Volunteer to present at a meeting and wing it. Offer to teach a local class on something you're passionate about. Form a support group. Find a place to stand up in front of others and speak.

3. Tell the truth. The friend with the annoying habit. The supervisor who favors the male staff. Your mother's callous commentary on your dating life. To have healthy relationships with others, we need honesty. But often, out of fear, we stifle what needs to be expressed. Process your feelings on your own first so you can be diplomatic. Then practice kind, healthy confrontation.

10

Don't Confuse the What for the Who

"WHY FIT IN, WHEN YOU WERE BORN TO STAND OUT."

—DR. SEUSS

Here's an experience I've had many times, and chances are you have too. There's a person I admire, usually in the public eye, whom I don't know directly. Normally, what I most admire is their creative gifts, what they've put out into the world. It could be a painting, song, or film. Maybe they've produced a book, business, or play. Whatever they've birthed in the world has moved, impressed, and thrilled me. It may even have motivated me to pick up a pen to produce something I wish to create! We all have our idols. It is at this point that I start to get confused. I confuse the what (that which has been created) with the who (the person who made it). This is entering a treacherous territory in which I am bound to be disappointed. The cliché "don't meet your heroes" is apropos here. There is no one living among us who is devoid of all that comes with the human experience. Everyone has flaws. Everyone has challenges. Yes, it may seem as if there are perfect people in the world. After all, many invest tremendous amounts of time, energy, and money into appearing perfect. But if a soul is inside a body, then it will be navigating the messiness of the human experience. The human body comes with physical limitations, emotions, and, an ego. Yes, even for that guru who publicly states they've transcended their ego. Every one of us will have areas of our lives that are easy and areas of growth that will be challenging. What comes easily and what we need to heal is unique for us all. There will be those who have the whole romantic-relationship thing figured out. And others for whom earning money will come very easily. But no one is given a universally perfect, pain-free, worry-free, all-successful life.

You meet the singer-songwriter of your favorite song. In your eyes, it's a perfect piece of artistry, and you deeply admire this person. Until you see them, inebriated, yelling at their assistant.

It's human nature to erect heroes, hoisting them up onto a pedestal, and to assume that that person has it all figured out. We assume that person is superior, gifted, and courageous. It's human nature to create gods out of mere mortals.

> **"PEOPLE TALK ABOUT BULLYING, BUT YOU CAN BE YOUR OWN BULLY IN SOME WAYS. YOU CAN BE THE PERSON WHO IS STANDING IN THE WAY OF YOUR SUCCESS, AND THAT WAS THE CASE FOR ME."**
>
> —KATY PERRY

Why Is This Important for the Misfit to Know?

The power that flows through you can do for you what feels impossible. I believe that the Universe is not separate from you. Not ever. Everything that makes up what you recognize about yourself and everything beyond comprehension is made up of one energy. One life. And that power is here to move through the filter that is you and to be expressed.

Not only should you not confuse the *what* for the *who* in others. Don't do this in yourself! Complicated, messy, awkward, flawed you is made of perfect stuff. Working with that perfection can help you achieve what you've never considered possible. This perfect stuff can heal your wounds, expand your courage, give you brilliant ideas, and attract your community of people. Perfect stuff can give you the right words at the right time. You find yourself sharing words that inspire or heal or confront and wonder, Where is this coming from? Inspiration does exist and it needs you to come through. Recognize that the vessel is the person. That's the who. And that person is having an imperfect human experience. At the same time, they are available for something extraordinary to be created through them. That's the what. The what is the Divine that was birthed through them, which is why it fills others with awe when they experience it. And you are just as capable of having it express through you too.

M2T Journal Moment

1. *When you see a person doing something extraordinary that inspires you, document this in your journal.*

Example: I heard the Billie Eilish song "Everything I Wanted" and felt so moved by it. The way she sings, the lyrics—it's just so perfect. She's a genius.

   Next, write this: The same energy that flows through them flows through me. It flows through everyone. They are unique and I am unique. This creative energy is within me and I am willing to let it flow. I am willing to let it express through me in my own way.

2. *Say the above affirmations or your own version of them. Repeat this mentally or even out loud when you encounter people who inspire you.*

M2T Exercise: Build Your Trailblazer Shrine

Surround yourself with images and items that represent the Trailblazer you are growing into. This sends powerful messages to the subconscious mind.

Rituals were an important part of everyday life in every known culture for thousands of years. It's only modern life that has cast aside this powerful tool to create change in this way. It's time to reclaim what has been discarded!

Rituals of healing or creation use small representatives to manifest a particular outcome in life.

Create a shrine to represent the Trailblazer you are growing into. This is a perfect daily reminder of who you truly are.

BUILDING YOUR SHRINE

Use items like photos, images, illustrations, postcards, cards (greeting, oracle, playing, game), statues, sculptures, toys, game pieces, figurines, rocks, crystals, candles, jewelry, natural objects like pinecones, dried branches, berries, reeds or flowers, feathers, kitchenware like glasses, small potted plants, books, tools, metal objects, fabric swatches, small clothing pieces like gloves or scarves, printed words or sentences, and much more. There are endless possibilities.

What's important is that this shrine represents you in all your uniqueness, not anyone else. I had a client who created an entire shrine from Pokémon cards. Another used only found objects and included a discarded doll and potato chip canister. One of my favorites was a student who made tiny figures from air-dry clay. She hadn't considered herself an artist but needed to get the specific ideas from her head into form.

Most of all, make this fun! It's not supposed to be a dreary chore. You're getting clearer about who you are now and who you came here to be. And now you're assembling artifacts to keep your focus and ease your transformation.

Be sure to include objects that represent:

1. *Who you are now*

   Keep it kind, please. Find a representative (rep) for your current state of being.

2. *The Trailblazer you are becoming*

   Find a rep for your Trailblazer. What does that version of yourself feel like? How do they behave? What challenges have they overcome?

3. *Your supporters*

   Both versions of yourself need support! Bring in representations for the people who see who you truly are. Family, friends, coworkers, community, club or church/synagogue/temple members.

   What if you don't feel you have any support? Add reps anyway. Or I should say, especially. If you were well supported, what would those folks be like? Unconditionally loving? Giver of accurate guidance? How about a creative partner? Someone to laugh with?

   This is a shrine inviting positive change. Making space for your ideal supporters on your shrine invites genuine people into your life.

4. *Your passions*

   What's most important to you? What makes life meaningful? That thing that gets you up in the morning?

5. *How you want to feel*

   How do you want to feel? Empowered? Strong? Confident? Invincible? Authentic, loving or compassionate?

6. *Make it sacred (or not)*

   Even though I'm using a spiritual word here, how sacred you make the shrine is up to you. I personally love using reps that enhance my connection to the Universe. My shrines have contained everything from deity statues to prayers, mantras, *affirmations, crystals, shamanic rattles, and temple bells. That represents me. You need to use what you feel comfortable with. A rep of your Higher Self can be extremely helpful.*

If you're sacred-light or completely avoidant, you may want to consider just adding a candle or two. Candles represent warmth and alchemy. Plus, lighting and extinguishing the candles brings action to an otherwise stationary collection. And most importantly, keeps your focus!

HOW TO USE YOUR TRAILBLAZER SHRINE

Feed it Your Attention

1. *Sit or stand before it.*

2. *Light a candle (if using).*

3. *Send love to your current representative.*

4. *Then focus your gaze on the Trailblazer rep. Imagine embodying this empowered version of yourself. Breathe into and expand that feeling.*

5. *Send love to your supporters—yes, including those who have not yet arrived.*

6. *Feel appreciation for your passions.*

Bring the Trailblazer Forward

1. *Start with your current rep and Trailblazer rep sitting side by side in the shrine.*

2. *Move the Trailblazer forward on the shrine, not blocking or eclipsing your current rep, but allowing the Trailblazer to progress be in the front.*

3. *Feel your Trailblazer expanding within you and leading all of you forward to empowerment.*

Doing this on the small scale will make it easier to create this in your life.

"I love that my friends are all freaks."
—DANIEL CRAIG

Cinema therapy is one of my favorite kinds of therapy! Watch M2T stories to uplift and inspire you.

Just please note that each of these creative acts were created during the time, culture, and consciousness of that year and that place in history. And this list represents a huge range in history. You may encounter jokes, plotlines, and characters that don't have the enlightened understanding we have today. Get what you're able to get from them and leave the rest.

The Matrix	*Stranger Than Fiction*
Napoleon Dynamite	*Edward Scissorhands*
Rudolph the Red-Nosed Reindeer	*Lilo and Stitch*
Frozen	*Meet the Robinsons*
Lucas	*Mask*
The Breakfast Club	*Thumbsucker*
Sixteen Candles	*Welcome to the Dollhouse*
West Side Story	*A Serious Man*
Lady Bird	*The Man Who Fell to Earth*
Lars and the Real Girl	*Harry Potter series*
Broken Flowers	*Muriel's Wedding*
Wadjda	*Eighth Grade*
Flirting	*Billy Elliot*
Everafter	*Dumplin'*
Field of Dreams	*Patti Cake$*
Garden State	*Never Have I Ever*
I Heart Huckabees	*Freaks and Geeks*

Blinded by the Light

Angus

Meatballs

The Bad News Bears

Unbreakable

Dodgeball: A True Underdog Story

Little Giants

Whip It

Bend It Like Beckham

Hairspray

Moonrise Kingdom

Pitch Perfect

Normal People

11

A Song Message for You

I'd been fretting over the book. This book. The very one I've been waiting to write for ten years—well, more like my whole lifetime. Now that the opportunity was here, sitting in my lap, marinating in my mind, could I find the right words? Would I say them in the best way possible? And *where were those words anyway?* I'd diligently sat at the computer over the months, coughed up lines and paragraphs, here and there, but the floodgates hadn't fully opened yet. I know that feeling when it does. *This ain't it.* Then one morning I awoke to a song playing in my head—clear, so familiar, but distant. That voice, that smokey, sultry voice, remarkable, inimitable, and yet I couldn't quite name her in the slow-to-start morning brain. Whatever this was, I hadn't heard it in a very long time. There was a vibration stirring in my heart, growing, pulsating strongly enough to rouse me from bed, and I stumbled down the hallway to my office. Laptop lid up. Blurry-eyeing up of the keys. Typing in the lyrics I was hearing and then, oh yes, of course, yes, it's Sade! No one else could ever sound like Sade. The song "By Your Side" began to play and brought forward an avalanche of tears. As Sade implored to the listener to cry, she would be there to wipe away the tears, and she would always be beside us! Here it was, a message from Spirit, softy chiding me for my doubts, reminding me that all the support I could ever need was right here. *It's always just right here.* I hadn't heard this song in decades, I thought, as I was flooded with sweet, nourishing relief: How often I'm forgetting divine timing, as I push, push, push, but that wasn't getting me what I wanted here. I felt my whole body sigh and let go, go, go. "I'll be there / By your side, baby." Message received.

I'm not alone. And I want you to know, you're not either. This message wasn't just for me. It's for you too.

Throughout this book I've shared about how to heal the Misfit within you so the Trailblazer inside can come alive. There's been the human side of healing, like in shifting your mindset and clearing old patterns and memories of pain. Then there's been the spiritual side of healing where I've spoken on the Universe, the nature of the soul and encouraged practices like prayer. In my decades of self-healing and my now fifteen years of my private practice, I have learned that deep restoration of our true self needs both approaches. We work with our minds and bodies to clear stuck emotional energy, calm the nervous system, and change our perceptions. We work with our spirits and the Great Spirit (that I mostly call the Universe here) to transcend the darkness, get inspired, and receive magical, magnificent support, opportunities, ideas, solutions, and so much love. Be sure to include both approaches in your own healing so those Extraordinary Ordinaries can become common occurrences for you.

M2T Journal Moment

1. Write about a song that touches your heart and makes you feel connected.

2. Can you think of a time a song "spoke" to you? What was happening and what did it tell you?

3. Write a few lines of lyrics or poetry as a message of encouragement from your Higher Self to the rest of yourself.

12

Cali Miracles

You know how we can learn from each other? Here's another story of something I experienced that I hope will resonate deeply within you.

I can start by saying, the California conference wasn't exactly *welcoming*. Sound familiar? (That seems to be a theme for me, doesn't it?) I had agreed to speak at a conference I was already scheduled to attend. The governing committee wasn't entirely convinced about what I had to offer, even though it had been they who had invited me. In meeting after meeting in the months leading up to this conference, it was made very clear: I was a side piece, an afterthought, not the star, and I better know my place. A far more renowned presenter would be who everyone was there to see. "No one there will know who you are," they said more than once, a warning for what was to come. And while it was true, I was new to this audience, I was certainly no stranger to speaking and presenting well to large groups of people. I tried to reassure them. "I'm going to do a great job." That felt like an old performance: trying to justify my spot in the room, in any room, to argue for my value. The entire conversation felt absurd. I mean, after all, *they* had asked *me* to do this, and here I was, mounting my defense, explaining all the reasons I deserved a place on that stage. If I hadn't been so stubborn, I would have pulled the plug and told them to go F themselves. But soon enough, all thoughts of this conference receded to the background of my life as a far more pressing concern had risen. My father, who had been going through unexpected health challenges, seemed to not be healing. I had a dream that he was leaving a formal event in a tuxedo. When I awoke, I knew that he wouldn't be making another comeback, that at some point soon he would be transitioning from this life into the next. To know this before he or anyone else did was devastating. From the stress, I developed odd health issues that no amount of specialists or tests could diagnose. Eventually my family became aware of what was happening. He wasn't interested in giving up, the stubbornness very much a family trait, and continued to work out at the gym until two weeks before he died, acting as if extra reps on the machines would beat the inevitable. A month before the conference, a week before I was moving, he left this earth, much faster than even I had expected. I scrambled to get all my belongings into my new place, threw sheets on the bed, slapped up a shower curtain, and headed to Florida to help my mother with what I have come to call, The Final Bureaucracies. If you don't know this now, you likely someday will, that when a person close to you dies, there's a series of lasts to be done. Picking up copies of death certificates from your local health department. Visiting the Social Security office. The trip to the Department of Motor Vehicles. Informing the insurance company. All on top of funeral services, writing an obit, and spreading the news to people you love. It's horrific that at a time when one is least able to deal with the cold realities of bureaucratic systems, they must be navigated. I got back to New Jersey with two days to unpack, do laundry, and repack for this conference. I woke up that morning, snot streaming out of my nose, my throat as if it were filled with knife blades, so painful to speak above a whisper. Why didn't I just cancel? I'm not sure. The Powers That Be would have been relieved, I'm sure, to not have had to deal with me. But my Higher Self (intuition) said, "Go." I threw random mismatched items in a suitcase and heaved myself onto the plane. (For the record, this was prior to the COVID-19 pandemic.) A few of the conference planners dismissed me as I entered the hotel lobby. I approached anyway: "I need to get to a pharmacy or health food store. I feel just awful." They dismissively suggested a cab. I knew immediately I was very much on my own here, that there would be no offers of assistance.

One thing I've noticed in talking with Misfits over the years is how we can become experts in independence and steering ourselves to meet our own needs, even in the most stressful times. It just seems easier to rely on ourselves than others. I felt horrible, but I knew I was up for this challenge! An eighty-dollar cab ride later, I procured a dozen bottles of water, herbal tea, vitamins, honey, and a handful of lemons. I was way behind on prepping for my presentation and sat down at the desk in my hotel room. It was then that I discovered that my laptop was dead and I lost access to all my notes. Oh boy, this was going to be fun.

Over the next two days, I glided through the conference, not fully present. After my initial rejection from the only people I knew there, the committee members, I had quickly connected with a man named Gary, a former longtime New Yorker, with an infectious laugh. The day before my talk, the star had done a lengthy presentation. I remembered looking around at the faces in the room, all clearly pleased. I felt more alone than ever. They had been right after all. This was *not* my audience. I thought much of the information they presented was surface level with commonly known information. And more than a few bits shared would be contradicted by my talk the next morning! If this was what this audience wanted, a speaker overflowing with meme-like platitudes and plastic positivity, then they were going to *hate* me.

I couldn't change my presentation. The slides had been emailed in two weeks before and I didn't have a working computer anyway. I remember digging in my conference bag for a journal and marker to at least jot a few new notes. The marker was dry! I said, "You've got to be kidding me!" as I threw it across the room. I gave up. "You just can't win every time. You can't always be lovingly received. You've got to fail sometime and that time is now. And you're still gonna get up on that stage and say what you came here to say."

Giving up can be incredibly freeing. I consoled myself a bit by saying, "These aren't your people. You'll never see them again." Rather than rehearsing, I spent the evening having fun downtown, pretending I was a tourist instead of being there for business. The next morning, I combed through my suitcase, realizing I hadn't brought any "show" apparel and pulled a not entirely flattering outfit together from what was still clean. Remember, I was not only sick but also still reeling from the loss of my father. I could've gotten mad at myself for not packing correctly, for not having a spare set of notes, or for any other number of things. I just didn't have the energy for any of that. In those moments, the best thing we can do for ourselves is give ourselves grace and remember, "Hey, I'm doing the best I can under these circumstances." Can you relate to that? What are times when you have had to give yourself some grace? How did that feel versus being hard on yourself?

So there I was, getting ready to go on stage and give my presentation. Next to the stage was a massive screen for the slides. I was standing beside it when one of the male attendees approached me. He looked at the screen, then at me, then back to the screen. Pointing at my headshot, he said, "Hardly looks like you!" With my messy hair, ill-fitting dress, and Rudolph-red stuffy nose, I of course knew this was true. But gee, I thought, what a way to kick a lady when she's down! The indignities continued. The emcee stood at the front to introduce me and, rather than reading my short bio, looked down at his feet, then over to me, back to the audience, and mumbled, "Uh, this next speaker is . . . um, well . . . she'll just tell you who she is." I thought, "Are you freaking kidding me?! My intuition brought me here for this shit?!" And then it was showtime!

I got on stage and the stuffy nose and scratchy throat instantly disappeared. I'd had this happen before, where I'm terrified that physical symptoms will disrupt something really important I need to do. Then *poof* I'm fine. Professional performers, like theater actors, often have similar stories to share. For me it meant something far beyond mind over matter. I had felt this before too. My Spirit was taking over my humanness, and right on time!

I introduced myself and immediately came clean to the audience. Rather than pretend I was a perfect person, living the perfect life, like the other presenters, I told them about the previous few months of unknown illness, my father's death, the move into a new place I'd spent only a few days in, only to arrive with a broken laptop. I said, "You may be asking yourselves what I'm even doing here. I've been asking myself that too. My Spirit said to come, so come I have. But I remembered something crucial just as my feet landed on this stage. I know, without a doubt, that no matter what is happening in my world, my Spirit is not limited by it! And my Spirit is what will be speaking with you today." With that, I was tuned in and turned on by what I came to share.

What transpired over the next ninety minutes was astonishing. I didn't utter a single "um." Information came through me to supplement what I had planned.

An exercise I led the audience through was a rousing success. I worked all angles of the stage and every eye was on me.

And the teaching I had been dreading, where I essentially gave information that contradicted the fluffy sentiments from the day before? I went for it. I was all in!

I acknowledged the ways we can harm others with spiritual truths. Humanness comes with pain at times. I had observed over and over how a person who is experiencing a loss or worrying financial matters or going through a breakup could be greeted with "Everything happens for a reason" or "It's all working out for your highest good" or "God is meeting your every need." I had witnessed countless times how this shuts down emotional energy and makes people feel shamed for having a natural reaction. In the past, I had of course been both the recipient and perpetrator of this. That's why I recognized how insensitive it was at best, and how ineffective and harmful it could be at worst.

I jokingly said, "Now I know no one here does that," as I scanned across the room, one eyebrow up, and smiling as I looked at their faces. A hushed, nervous chuckling followed my roving gaze. I had called them out, gently, and they were receiving it.

I made it clear: Meet people where they are! True healing comes from compassion first and compassion always. Greet people and their pain with empathy and understanding rather than by throwing out a bunch of clichés. It is important to deal with your own emotional pain so you can hold a safe space for others that are experiencing it. Save the spiritual guidance, education, and practices for a time when it can be best received. They got it. I was encouraging us all to bring even more light into the world, ironically, by acknowledging, rather than denying, the darkness. It's only then that we can open the door and let the light in, as we extend our hands, reaching out, to help show others a way out.

I delivered what had been mine to say. That couldn't have been delivered by anyone else, any other way. I had slayed the dragons of my own insecurities and old wounds to fulfill a sacred mission.

I finished to a resounding standing ovation! Electricity and light, vibrations of ecstasy, a pulsing euphoria encompassed me so completely that I could have floated down to the floor. The emcee yelled at me from the front of the stage and said, "Don't move! Stay there! We're gonna do a Q and A!" We are? They didn't want me to leave! Answering questions for about ten minutes, I finally exited the stage and ballroom, in hot pursuit of a snack. I never eat before a talk and, as is customary, was now famished. My job was complete. What I thought would be my ultimate failure ended up a rousing success in every way!

When I came into the back of the room, the star was ready for their next presentation. They saw me and said, "How about another big round of applause for Kris Ferraro!" Now that was a first—a second standing ovation!

Then something absolutely otherworldly happened. I should say, something *else* otherworldly, as the biggest miracle had just happened. If you aren't a spiritual person, you may have to just go with me on this one, as this is what I experienced. As the star was speaking, I saw something leave them, a form, and slowly float through the room headed in my direction. This form looked like a long, clear, thin sword-like shape that took on the colors in the room as it passed through. I had noticed something moving, but had no idea what I was seeing, I couldn't turn my eyes away. This form reached about three feet from where I was standing. Being an energy healer, I know how to create a bubble of protection around me whenever I'm out in public. Whatever this was hit my shield and fell to the floor, shattering into what looked like thousands of grains of gray sand! I looked down at my feet, at these tiny pieces of dense energy, as they scattered and were absorbed by the floor. It was the most incredible thing I had ever seen!

There are many mystics who can see things in the unseen realm. That's not my gift. In my entire lifetime, I've probably seen ten dead people and a handful of animals in spirit form. I feel everything, yet don't see much. And although I energetically protect myself every day, I had never *seen* that system in action. I just know protecting my sensitivities makes me *feel* much better, so I continue to do it.

My light had ruffled a few feathers. Your light will do that too. And you'll be so happy, it won't even faze you for a moment.

The awe I had already been feeling, from having succeeded when I was convinced I would fail, multiplied by a hundred in that moment. All I could keep thinking was, This is so cool! This is incredible! I can't believe this happened!

And the most miraculous part of this whole story? Yes, bigger than my success, more surprising than my mystical experience? After I left

the stage, I was embraced by all the people I had felt rejected by. A true healing had happened instantaneously. We had been projecting our own stuff onto one another. Once that was healed, we could truly see one another and there was nothing there but love. One at a time, over the course of the rest of the event, most committee members told me my presentation was outstanding. And I didn't gloat, not one bit. And the sword thrower? I loved them too. I know what it's like to feel upstaged or get jealous. They're an incredibly accomplished and successful person. If I upset them, then I must be doing something right!

LETTER TO MY YOUNG MISFIT

Hey there, cutie,

You've been going through so much. I know that. There's so many times you felt different than everyone else. And you've been getting the message that different is wrong. What you don't know is that anyone who has ever done anything worthwhile in this big world felt exactly like you. And I want you to know, you are loved. Not just loved, you are love itself, exactly as you are. There's a movement called It Gets Better. And that movement is right on! You're going to grow and heal, learn and share, and be introduced to a bigger life than you've ever known before. You're going to find your people, baby. And you're going to catch the world on fire in a way only you can. I can't wait!

I love you so much,

Your Trailblazer

13

Finding Your People

As I've mentioned, the Misfits of the world become very comfortable being alone. It can come so naturally. No competing with others' needs. No being swayed by another's mood. For others, the experience of comfort in aloneness has been less organic. The harsh behaviors of others have led you to mistrust and avoid too much togetherness. With either inclination, it's just plain easier to not have to explain yourself to people, which is exhausting and futile.

So you may be asking, *What's there to heal here? Why go from what is comfortable and safe to what may not be? Why find my people?*

Because, dear readers, our biology is designed for community and companionship. We are intended for connecting with others, for shared tasks, and for being in service to one another. Even for introverts. Even for those who've been rejected or ridiculed. There are more people living alone right now than has ever existed in history and the all-important studies say this is a very bad thing.

I currently live alone—well, not counting Ling and The Baby Cheetah, my two beloved cats. At the same time, I've formed a community with my neighbors in the apartment building we share. We help one another in a myriad of ways: carrying heavy boxes, watching one another's pets, sharing food, supporting one another's businesses. A few months ago, when I unexpectedly came down with strep throat, my neighbor Thomas went shopping for me, returning with those extra soft tissues and other sickbed necessities. When there's a problem in the building, we join forces to communicate our needs to the landlords. We have each other's backs. I'm also a part of a beautiful (and local) spiritual community, where we love one another deeply, praying for and supporting one another in every conceivable way. And if anything major occurred, I can count on at least twenty friends within a ten-mile radius who would pop up immediately for me, without question or complaint, even in the middle of the night. This is my local family of choice and they give me a great sense of security, warmth, love, and joy.

It certainly wasn't always this way. There were years of my life when I felt completely isolated and on my own. Then there were times when my community was only global, rather than local. Technology is brilliant in enabling us to connect across the miles. There are so many people I dearly love who happen to live all over the world. I cherish my ability to connect with and know them. They just can't pick me up if I have a flat tire. I made a very conscious decision to create a local, diverse community. To deepen easy acquaintances into more fulfilling friendships. To chitchat in the hallways instead of rushing about my business. To show up for others. To ask for help and see who's willing. And to be vulnerable and ask for help in the first place. To risk being ignored or rejected. Many people see me, time and again, rise up after setbacks, stand in my truth, and muscle my way through challenges—at times,

> **"A DEEP SENSE OF LOVE AND BELONGING IS AN IRREDUCIBLE NEED OF ALL PEOPLE. WE ARE BIOLOGICALLY, COGNITIVELY, PHYSICALLY, AND SPIRITUALLY WIRED TO LOVE, TO BE LOVED, AND TO BELONG. WHEN THOSE NEEDS ARE NOT MET, WE DON'T FUNCTION AS WE WERE MEANT TO. WE BREAK."**
>
> —BRENÉ BROWN

gracefully; at other times, not so much. They see me teaching others how to do the same. I have not one but three Wonder Woman mugs that were given to me by people who somehow see me just that way. But I have as much need for support as anyone. Sometimes this Wonder Woman feels like a Little Lost Girl or Helpless Victim or the Last Picked. Wonder Woman gets all the good press. It makes sense. She's got those raven locks, a tiny waist, and that cool shield. She's 100 percent fearless! But I am not. I have my own badassery, and those times are often my most visible. And there are vulnerable parts of me that need assistance and compassion. I had to learn to let all my flaws and weaknesses be seen.

Now you may be a Misfit with a romantic partner, children, other close family, and friends from high school or college. If you don't feel as if you can be completely, 100 percent yourself and are deeply understood by them, it's time to move out of your comfort zone, which provides a solid foundation, a home base, to expand upon. You're still going to need your people, the ones who truly get unique you.

Here's why finding (and creating) your own sacred circle of people is important.

Loneliness

Loneliness is a deep ache that doesn't get solved by being around another person. It feels fulfilled when we experience deep emotional intimacy with another. Finding your people gives you the opportunity to be seen and to see.

Companionship

Even the most introverted introvert needs to be around other people at times for things like fun! Shared experiences. Laughing. Talking the small talk (I was never a fan but have since come around). Being human with other humans.

Experience Others' Ideas and Perspectives

In our modern world, we can easily curate a friend group, a social media feed, and a following—all based on shared perspectives. I keep hearing a great deal of relationships being held together by "agreeing to disagree." I agree that this is sometimes what is necessary. It's easier. It's gentler. It allows you to move in specific social situations safely. In some cases, it's the only choice. Just please know it also limits those relationships. I'm not sure when everyone universally decided to only have others in their lives who agree with them. It certainly hasn't seemed to have created a more peaceful world.

Here's a bit of a hard truth. We need people. And we need people who can offer ideas, perspectives, information, and solutions we can't resource on our own. Your people can do just this, if you're open enough to receive them. What's important for your people is that you share many of the same values.

> **"ENCOURAGING SOMEONE TO BE ENTIRELY THEMSELF IS THE LOUDEST WAY TO LOVE THEM."**
>
> —KALEN DION

Perspectives Versus Values

Rather than shared perspectives, I'd like to see you focus on the importance of shared values. Two people can both value freedom, for example. But they each vote for opposing political candidates. Or love is an important value. There's just lots of ways to love.

Get Told About Yourself

There are aspects of ourselves we cannot see. Ways we are getting in our own way. Ways we are sabotaging the very opportunities we've been waiting for. The human experience comes with behaviors that can push others away. Or harm ourselves or others. How will we know unless another tells us? I've literally spent three decades delving into my conscious and subconscious minds. I pride myself on having a high level of self-awareness. Part of that comes with just plain awareness. When I'm fully here, wherever that may be, moment by moment, I take in a great deal of not-obvious information. And to keep growing, expanding, and dream building, I still need to be told about myself at times. I have qualities and commit acts of sabotage that I just don't realize. Deep friendships at times can involve (compassionately) saying the hard things, offering alternative perspectives (one of our M2T gifts), and helping the other person get out of their own way. This enables them to do the same for you.

Heal the Sting of Past Rejections

This book has given you many opportunities to heal the past hurts. Now that the wounds are cleaned out, time with your people seals the healing in by filling it with love.

Create a Movement

The truth is you can achieve much more with others. 1 + 1 = the power of wherever 2 or more are gathered. Use your shared values (see next) to combine forces to do good for others. You can be a part of creating great social and creative change. More peace. A cleaner environment. Greater safety for everyone who needs it. Overflowing creativity. You can do all this; you just can't do it alone.

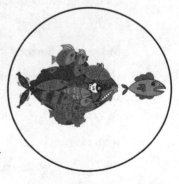

The Most Important Step to Finding Your People: Move from Interests to Values

Misfits who become Trailblazers can have unconventional interests when it comes to music, movies, art, spirituality, lifestyle, food, and more. Our interests can demonstrate what makes us passionate about being alive.

During a holiday gathering, your similar-aged cousins' conversation turns to the series *Riverdale* while you'd like to gush about *I Am Not Okay with This*. You haven't seen their show and they haven't seen yours, so you end up feeling left out. You could easily hop online and find other fans of your show. That's a fun way to connect.

Whether it's a passion for furry-dragon fursonas, classic Japanese anime, steampunk-crafting regalia, Civil War reenacting, heritage microbreweries, *Game of Thrones* skater fans, gay goths with *My Little Pony* tattoos, driving vintage dune buggies on the beach, living in off-the-grid treehouses—there is literally a collective for every type of interest and subinterest. It's never been easier to find your folks. They're just a Google search away. Well, except for maybe the off-the-grid treehouse dwellers. They might not have Wi-Fi.

Just don't let your interests be the only defining factor of your people. It's absolutely uplifting to share your passions with others. And you're going to need a whole lot more than that to experience true connection.

Move from Surface Interest to Shared Values

Core values define what is most important to you and can guide important decisions, including deciding whom to spend time with.

Here are a few of mine:

HONESTY

Like many empaths, I'm a human lie detector. Energetically, I mostly know when people aren't being truthful, and this makes me uncomfortable. I would rather a friend say to me, "I can't meet you tonight after all because I now have a date," than make up an excuse. When a person in my life is honest with me, even when it's not what I want to hear, I know I can trust them.

SAFETY

I do everything in my power to make others around me feel safe, and I need the same in return. While no one can take responsibility for my triggers, I can choose to spend time with people who understand themselves well and choose to be gentle, direct, and kind with me. During the early COVID days, I made a very clear choice to spend time with people I felt safe with, which meant backing off of or even ending relationships with people I didn't. It was a decision that ensured the spaces left open were filled with exactly the kind of people I felt the most at ease with. Best. Decision. Ever.

OPEN-MINDEDNESS

An essential for most Misfits who become Trailblazers. Throughout my life, I have worked diligently to suspend my snap judgments and see beyond the most common viewpoints. Early on in my spiritual journey, I had to suspend disbelief long enough to explore outwardly "wacky" practices. Many of those same wacky practices I'm teaching today! It also enabled me to learn more about differing people's beliefs and behaviors. Now I can connect with people from all over the world, exactly where they are.

What are your core values? Here is list of forty common ones to get you started:

1. Accountability
2. Balance
3. Beauty
4. Bravery
5. Commitment
6. Compassion
7. Creativity
8. Dependability
9. Diversity
10. Empathy
11. Exploration
12. Fairness
13. Faith
14. Flexibility
15. Freedom
16. Gratitude
17. Growth
18. Honesty
19. Humility
20. Humor
21. Integrity

22. Kindness

23. Love

24. Loyalty

25. Mindfulness

26. Open-mindedness

27. Originality

28. Passion

29. Peacefulness

30. Resilience

31. Respect

32. Safety

33. Sensitivity

34. Spirituality

35. Strength

36. Support

37. Thoughtfulness

38. Trust

39. Uniqueness

40. Wisdom

> **"YOU ARE HERE AS THE CREATIVE SOLUTION AND NOW IS YOUR TIME TO SERVE."**
>
> —DR. SUE MORTER

M2T Journal Moment

1. *Start with the question: What values mean the most to me? Close your eyes, take a deep breath, and silently repeat the question a few times, leaving space in between.*

2. *Think of the values you least like in others and write them here. Examples: stinginess, selfishness, and superficiality.*

3. *What are the positive opposites of these? Examples: generosity, selflessness, and depth.*

4. *Think of a person you greatly admire. It can be someone you know or a public figure. What values do you believe they possess? Ask if these are yours as well.*

5. *Do an internet search on values. There are hundreds out there. Use this to get you started in creating your own list.*

14

Too Freaking Big

A couple of days after I submitted the first draft of this manuscript, I drove a few hours to connect with a small gathering of friends.

Much of my summer had been spent in a tiny, historic local library, writing and dreaming and unearthing my own shaky fears about being this vulnerable in print. I had been mentally moving through the timeline of my life, revisiting all the places I've most experienced the pain of being excluded, along with the triumphant elation of how I've flourished, not only in spite of, but at times because of this exclusion. Memories that had been discarded soon after they happened came back to me in blazing detail. There were the enemies who held me down. There were all the angels who taught and encouraged me. A deeper understanding emerged. This, all of it, every single bit of it, has been a necessary part of my path. What a revelation! This wasn't just a concept, but now a deeply embodied truth. Writing this book strapped me into an emotional roller-coaster ride, with drops, dips, and swirls I hadn't anticipated. My body pushed back with strange symptoms for which there was no medical explanation. These would divert my attention, temporarily, and then I'd return to the pages, more committed than ever to bringing this information out to anyone who could benefit. My body would quiver, saying, "Why are you *doing* this? It's not safe." I'd do my best to reassure by saying, "I hear you. I know you're scared. We haven't always had support. But there are so many people out there who've been made to feel wrong and bad. They don't know who they really are. We are here to let them know. This is important, sacred, holy work." (My body still isn't completely convinced. We're working on it.)

After months spent navigating this difficult terrain, I was feeling depleted, and more than a bit concerned. As far as rough drafts go, this one was rougher than most, and the perpetual good girl in me who still wants to do everything perfectly wasn't pleased. I had been putting enormous pressure on myself. Must. Say. Everything! Must. Say it. Right! Listen, I know better. I have expert-level experience in cutting-edge tools to dissipate just such creativity-killing energy as this. But there were times when I couldn't get out of my own way, regardless.

I was looking forward to downtime, catching up, and sweet laughter, craving the easy warmth of like-minded beloveds I can't ever seem to get enough of.

On the morning of this gathering, I woke up with a serious and strange stomachache. Not wanting to cancel, I sat down to conduct energy work to get clarity and clear it. There it was again. That feeling of absolute fear. An image came into my awareness of Clark, another attendee. I assumed it was based on a couple of confusing past experiences I had had with him over the years. My stomach calmed, and I readied myself for the drive.

My hosting friend, Brenda, and the others greeted me with huge hugs. Just what I needed! Clark would be the last to arrive. I was looking out the window when he pulled in. Although there were many parking options, he pulled in right behind my car, blocking me in. My stomach twisted again, which I quickly ignored. After all, I *was* genuinely happy to see him too.

At lunch, sitting in my friend's elegant dining room, another attendee asked about this book. I knew it would be beneficial to share because I needed encouragement and support. As I started to speak, Clark cut me off. I wasn't surprised, as I had been in group settings with him before. He often brought the focus of attention back to himself. (I'm betting you know someone like this too.) And, honestly, I was too tired to be annoyed and just let it pass. I do my best to accept people as they are and not take much personally these days. We had hours together. I could share later.

After eating, as we sat on a circular sectional sofa in the living room, Clark across from me, he once again commandeered the group's focus.

"I have something to say. I'm taking a class about bringing uncomfortable feelings out in the open." Uh-oh—my stomach lurched. Here we go. Looking at me directly, he continued, "And I just have to say this. Kris, you're just too big sometimes! Your voice is too big. You're too loud. Your energy is too big. It's just *something* about you. It's overbearing. It makes me uncomfortable. I've been feeling this way for a while. And now I can't be present because of you."

I felt completely blindsided. My heartbeat started to race as my temples began to drip with sweat. Having already arrived compromised, it wasn't surprising I was going into a full-blown shock response. My face flushed deep red with humiliation and my mind flashed to his car blocking mine. In the battle of fight vs. flight, flight was here. It took every bit of self-control to not shoot up, grab my purse, and run out of there, peeling out on my friend's lawn to escape. Adding to it was feeling the pain of everyone else there too. They were stunned and embarrassed for me. Immediately, from the overwhelm, I exploded with searing hot tears.

The little girl in me started to scramble, wanting to make everything okay for Clark, along with the rest of the crew. And although my inner child spoke first, she didn't speak loudly or have the final word. My empowered inner grown-up stepped forward resolutely. She spoke to me, "Wait a minute! This isn't your fault! This has *nothing* to do with you."

A seismic shift happened inside me. My voice, grounded, clear, and strong came through. "Now *I'm* going to be honest. I want to leave. I didn't come here for this. I'm not taking your class, Clark, where you all must have some boundaries or rules around confrontation. I didn't agree to this. And I'm not responsible for your insecurities and weaknesses. I'm not responsible for your feelings and failings. I get triggered by other people too. *We all do.* But I don't subject those people to my pain. I do my work, and then if there needs to be a conversation, I'll have it from a clean space. I know to do this. *Why don't you?* I'm not here to make you feel comfortable or change myself to make you feel comfortable. I don't have any control of that. Yes, I'm big and my energy is always going to be big. And by the way, as you are a thin person, telling me I'm 'too big' is not okay. Even though you weren't speaking about my body, it's still just not okay to do this."

I stood up for myself, speaking my truth. And took all the crap being thrown at me and volleyed it right back to where it belonged, with him.

The sensation of elation and freedom that followed will be with me forever. The most exquisite natural high was unleashed. My nervous system, sensing my defense, let out an exhale, and came back into balance, knowing the threat had passed.

The most incredible experience followed. My friend Angela began to speak. She talked about her own experience, how she too felt blindsided by this. She shared how she had been so looking forward to seeing me and how happy she was I came. Brenda talked about how she felt an enormous responsibility to create peace within the group. At the same time, her protective mama bear energy had been activated when she saw my hurt. Angela and Brenda came to where I was sitting and embraced me. And I let down my guard and let myself be showered in love, compassion, and support.

Brenda, a true healing pro, then led us all through a profound healing process. As healers, we walk our walk. Clark got clear that I was triggering feelings he had about a sibling who'd been the star of the family. I also got clear. The day before, on social media, I had seen a post by Suzanne Evans, a highly successful marketing expert, business owner, and coach, who also happens to be a full-figured woman. Normally sharing content-rich and funny materials, I was shocked to see that she had posted her photo and pasted over it with nasty troll insults about her size. Doesn't matter that she is a successful and hilarious speaker, teacher, mother, and coach and is running a profitable business. No, for some people it will always come down to appearance. Deeply disturbed, I quickly scrolled past it. I didn't realize. It had stuck. That thirty-second scroll pause had gotten in. Out of our clearing process, a thought spoke loudly: *Wait until this happens to you. Wait until people talk about how big you are.* If Clark hadn't said what he had, I wouldn't have known that was rolling around inside me.

On a human level, I was also clear about what had happened in that room.

His need for presence was more important than my need for respect and safety.

His inability to recognize and manage his own triggers disrupted my ability to be open and vulnerable.

His lack of boundaries trampled on my commitment to fully be myself, "big-ness" and all.

So here's an open confession, dear readers:

Clark is right.

I've always been TOO BIG.

My body.

My brain.

My beauty.

My boldness.

My bravery.

My creativity, my compassion, my sensuality, my love.

My integrity, my honesty, my drive to heal and be healed. My commitment to knowing the great mystery intimately.

My sensitivity and intensity. Yep. That too.

And the biggest "too big" thing about me? My heart.

Too, too much.

Each and every bit of it. Too freaking BIG.

I've been too big for too many people for too damn long. There have been a lot of people who've felt threatened. Lovers, coworkers, friends, even complete strangers haven't known what to do with such Bigness.

But those aren't my people.

And I'm done. I'm done apologizing. I'm done trying to change myself for anyone but myself.

And that, dear readers, is what I most want for you.

There will always be people who look at you like you're too much or not enough of something. There will be plenty, keen to lean in and inform you what they feel is wrong or off about you, how you don't meet their standards. How *you* need to change to make *them* feel better. There are entire industries built on just this. All of this feedback is based on their judgments, biases, wounds, limitations, and histories.

Your light is going to highlight the insecurities and inadequacies of others. The only way they can feel safe and equal is to point out your "flaws." To make you wrong, less than, or weird.

And all of this, each and every little bit, needs to get filed under "Not My Freaking Problem." Immediately. As soon as you've been sprayed with the Super Soaker of Conformity and Mediocrity. As soon as your bigness is bombarded by smallness. Remember: "Oh yeah, this isn't my freaking problem! Let me just stick it in that file, dry myself off, and keep going."

Because those aren't your people. Your people *are* out there.

Clark just wasn't able to be my people. Not that day anyway. He was at one time. But not now and possibly not ever again. In the aftermath of what I said, he was able to apologize and own his stuff. I know it was sincere. In the moment he said what he said, he had no idea that he was hurting me along with the rest of the group. May be hard to imagine that, but we're all living from inside our own experience and there are times each and every one of us is just plain clueless, especially when we feel activated. Clark and I both did our work, processing what came up and later going outside to ground our energy. Everyone stayed and enjoyed the rest of the day. Clark may look like an enemy. But he was an angel who showed me my hidden fear and, ultimately, just how strong, powerful, and healthy I am. What I said in that room was as much a declaration to the Universe and everyone in it as it was to him. I've been walking taller and more confidently ever since.

Then there are my other friends. That day, they defended and surrounded me with compassion, solace, and love. Holding space, they helped usher in the healing that took place for me and Clark. Not intimidated by my growth, they encourage and celebrate it.

Those are my people.

I want you to find your people and feel this kind of deep connection too.

On the long drive home, more exhausted than ever from all that emotional intensity, I kept the music off and let myself be enveloped by the soothing sounds of the rain. When I was twenty minutes from home, Angela called to check in on me. There it was again. Even more love. More support. Together, we both ranted and laughed. I told her I kept imagining Brenda's spouse arriving home that night and innocently asking her, "So, how did it go?" And this had us both in stiches! I said, "You really surprised me. Thank you so much for what you shared. For standing up for me. I can't even put into words how much that meant." She replied, "I just took a page from your book, Kris." And together, we cried. Beautiful, poignant tears this time. We cried for ourselves and for one another for how much we've healed, how much we've grown. For how we've learned to show up and stand up for ourselves. And for the times that ignites the bravery in others to do the same. We were both filled with immense warmth.

When one rises, it invites *everyone* to rise. This sums up exactly why I wrote this book and why I'm sharing this personal experience here.

I want you to take a page from my book, from *this* book, both literally and figuratively.

And RISE.

Rise up out of the wounds of the past. Forgive them, Universe, for they know not what they do.

Rise up from broken-down ideas about who you were told to be.

Rise up out of the shame and pain of the conditioning.

Rise up and STAND UP for yourself and others. There are so many sweet souls who need you!

Rise up toward everything that feels right and true for you. Follow what resonates.

Rise up in the direction of new possibilities. They're calling you forward.

Rise up for the dreams awaiting to be born through you. You will be supported in unexpected ways.

Rise up to the urgings and callings of your one precious soul. It's time.

Be too big, too much, too radical, too weird, too passionate, too intense!

Get so comfortable with the dimensions of yourself that you can maintain this when greeted by the discomfort you arouse in others.

Love yourself so much that you can also love people who project their pain onto you. Usually this works best at a distance.

Let the true you become the only you.

Blaze a trail forward like *only you can*. You will be assisted and guided. This support, divine and otherwise, just can't show up until you do.

Show up for strange, mysterious, and wonderous you.

The best is before you.

Your visions, birthed through you.

Your people, understanding you.

Your freedom, liberating you.

It's all awaiting your yes. Let the M2T expedition begin.

Conclusion

It's the last week in August 2022 and I'm ensconced in a tiny little library that hardly anyone visits. It's very old, with a cathedral ceiling and skyscraper windows that let in the expansive summer sun. It's been a friendly writing space for this book, offering the gentle safety and potent silence needed for focus.

It's obvious to me that whenever I'm feeling lost or scattered, I am automatically drawn back to the library. The endless search of self-discovery started in a preinternet era when I was a tiny girl, with the questions "Who am I?" and "Why am I different?" explored at my local small-town library. It was there at eight years old that I inquired why there weren't more books on the Loch Ness monster. After all, I had already read the three they had. I think back and marvel at the kindness and acceptance bestowed upon me there, a clearly odd child exasperated with the limits of both a tiny town and readily available monster information. I wanted answers! There would be more books to explore on psychic powers and astrology, meditation and miracles, years before I could understand what any of that would mean for me personally. Paging through books written for adults, I found many words and concepts beyond my understanding, yet I was drawn to them anyway, as if I could absorb the information through osmosis. I especially liked the ones that had illustrations, diagrams, and photos. I remember a drawing of a woman with a bubble around her, her aura encased in an energetic shield. For some reason, it made sense to me, although I could not have told you what I was seeing. The seventies was a time of bucking conventions with radical exploration. A genuinely good time for a weird little girl to come back to earth.

These thoughts are disrupted by an unusual sound coming from right outside. Is that a *saxophone*? Then a full band joins in, and I'm having one of those moments when I feel as if I've stumbled into an alternate reality. A live band? Playing outside the *library*? *This forgotten library?*

A staff member tells me it's the last week of Music Mondays, a summer library program. And I start to laugh. *Of course it is.*

Donning earbuds playing diurnal beats, I write for a bit longer, then pack up to head out, in search of an uncrowded coffee shop, perhaps, or another quiet spot. As I descend the many stone steps, I am face to face with about fifty townspeople, dancing and swaying, heads bopping to the music, while children twirl on the grass, blowing bubbles and laughing. And it's all just too perfect.

My neighbors are savoring the languid, lazy, hazy last days of summer before the return to school and work, and autumn descends. They're in unscheduled bliss. Time off. Vacation mode. Fun times and gentle movement.

For me, the summer of 2022 has been all about *Your Difference Is Your Strength*. If I wasn't writing, I was thinking about it, and when I wasn't thinking, I was talking about it, seeing signs of what to include reflected everywhere, gleaning insights from others Misfits while my ADD brain did its best to capture each insight. I've never written in a linear format. Instead, my books are formed as puzzle pieces, with multiple documents that in the end will be put into order and clicked into place. While the people around me are in the external joy of summer, I've been incubating, creating, and birthing this book. That in the final stretches I am confronted with how out of resonance with the rest of the world I am makes perfect sense. There would have been a time when that reminder would have made me feel alone or freakish. The dreaded FOMO could have roused its big-eyed head, searching for the greener grass, making me feel left out.

Instead, I'm so deliciously happy right here, exactly where I am, in full productivity mode, sharing what means the most to me. I never take it for granted.

After kids have returned to school and everyone else is back at work, this book will be completed, and a summer of my own making will begin. There will be a week at a beach with friends and family, morning swims, seashell-collecting walks, gentle afternoon naps, and nothing on my schedule but joy. My time is in its right time. It doesn't have to coincide with the crowd. In fact, it never will.

For now, I ask myself, in this, my long love letter to you, my sweet M2Ts, is there anything else I want you to know? Is there anything I alluded to rather than spelled out? Are there any points I really want to drive home?

I Want You to Know You Are Loved

Exactly as you are right now. With your obvious differences and the ones no one sees. With your history and inconsistencies and misgivings. With your diagnoses and analyses. With the projections attached to you and the lies you've told to yourself about yourself. Through the confusion and fear, illusions and doubts, you are loved. Even with the mistakes you have made. You are made from a life force that is Love itself with the capital L. You can *only* be loved, no matter what. This love is infinite. This love is eternal. This love is your love, now and always.

Let the love in.

I Want You to Know You Are Known

Every pain you've ever endured. Every need unmet. Every desire never admitted, not even to yourself. Every gift you've been given, including those in dormancy. Every hair on your body. Every blood cell flowing through your veins. Every thought you've ever thought, every feeling you've ever felt. Every single possibility of the many possibilities for your future. Known.

Let that realization of being known in. Then let the Universe's knowing be yours. Let it guide you.

I Want You to Know You Are Supported

As your lungs are supported with oxygen from the trees. As the sun provides you with warmth. Every drop of water that hydrates, cools, and bathes you, supports you. Every morsel of food that touches your lips nourishes you. Every watt of electricity that provides light, fuels your toaster, brings your devices to life, gives to you. The earth beneath your feet houses and provides for you. The Universe has so much more to give to you.

Allow yourself to receive. Allow more support to flow through your life.

I Want You to Know You Are Valuable

Your unique presence. Your precious heart. There is no other you. All the wisdom from all the journeys your ancestors endured to give life to one-of-a-kind you. It's all within you. Your compassion for others. Your different ways of seeing. Your bravery and courage. How you keep moving forward, no matter what. The gifts you're not sure what to do with. The ones you wish you had distracting you from the right ones you do have. The ones still waiting to emerge. Your ability to choose to love yourself. Your ability to love others and love life.

Feel your inherent worth. And if you can't feel it, affirm it until you do.

I Want You to Know You Have a Purpose and a Mission

Yes, you. No matter where you are in your life right now. Still in school. Looking for a job. Hating a job. Leaving a marriage. Raising a child. Moving cross-country. Retiring. Stop waiting for the right or perfect time to begin. Stop waiting for the "grand mission" and just start serving now. What you need to know will be revealed when you need to know it.

If you're asking, "What can one person possibly do?" I have two perfect examples from my own life to show you. It would be easy enough to point out more well-beloved historical figures. But that may lead you to think, *Those people are rare* or *Those people don't exist anymore.* Nothing could be further from the truth.

After an early experience with EFT (emotional freedom techniques), more commonly known as Tapping, I knew I wanted to learn more about it. Twenty years ago, workshops were only in person, with very few practitioners teaching it, most often in places out of driving distance for me. Making it even more difficult for me to attend was the cost. At the time, I was struggling to support myself on a social-service salary. Then I learned of an EFT workshop being taught in Valley Cottage, New York, about forty-five minutes away. Suspiciously, the cost was for a donation of choice, which I had never heard of before. I was convinced it would be a scam, where I would be subjected to a time-share sales pitch or recruited for a cult. At the very least, I was sure it would be a poor-quality workshop with an inexperienced teacher. What I encountered instead blew my mind! The instructor was CJ Puotinen, an experienced holistic-health writer, who taught with clarity, enthusiasm, and purpose. She included lots of storytelling, and this is how I've always learned best. There were demonstrations and hands-on practice sessions. Once fully immersed in the fundamentals, I was hooked! I got to experience in real time that this odd-looking healing technique worked incredibly well for me. CJ was enormously generous with her time, knowledge, and expertise. There was a follow-up memo sent to all the participants with resources and opportunities to practice with tapping buddies. The workshop was so popular, it expanded to two and three days long, scheduled a few times throughout the year, for well over a decade! At times there would be up to ninety people in a room, all tapping and learning together, many of us arriving with enormous challenges in our health and in our financial and personal lives. No one was ever turned away. Each of us paid what we could. And those donations collected? Every cent funded a visiting-pet program to train therapy animals for nursing home and hospital visits. In other words, CJ taught the classes for free. At one point, tables were set up in the lobby where participants could bring books and other things they'd like to give away.

All were welcome to these secondhand treasures. Out of those classes, healings happened, miracles unfolded, friendships were made, and deep connections were forged. Many of us went on to become certified EFT practitioners, healing and teaching others, continuing an outreach of transformation and generosity. It's impossible to fathom the ripple effect CJ has had, just in this one area of her life. Hundreds of people attended over the years. And each one of those people went back to their lives with opened minds and hearts. I, for one, have now worked with thousands of clients and students. I have written hundreds of newsletters, thousands of social media posts, and two, soon to be three (!), books, all connecting back to her. And I'm just one person too!

And speaking of that early EFT experience, I have hypnotherapist Roxanne Louise to thank for that. In absolute crisis mode due to a traumatic breakup in my midtwenties, I newly entered therapy. At the same time, I decided to finally commit to the spiritual journey I've been aware of since early childhood. I somehow knew that this would be a key piece to my healing. What unfolded was a great period of exploration that led me to Roxanne. I had always known I had lived before, even though reincarnation was not a belief I was raised with or even heard of. Seemingly on a whim, I made an appointment for a past-life-regression session. If I had had any doubts upon entering, they were surely gone by the time I left. I reexperienced three lifetimes, including one with my bestie, Ulana, and another with the ex, which had given me great peace. The emotions that came up were very much real. Eventually, Roxanne introduced me to the powers of the subconscious mind, affirmations, the New Thought classic books of Catherine Ponder, and so much more. Again, all concepts, ideas, beliefs, skills, and practices that are completely integrated into my everyday life. Recently, I tracked Roxanne down after twenty-two years and was thrilled to find her still teaching and working with clients. I thought it odd to include information here in my book about how she's impacted my life without telling her directly. I sent her an email titled "Blast from the past!" I wanted her to know about what has transpired with one of her students, whom she hadn't seen in decades, me. Not sure she'd even remember me, I tried my best to explain her impact on every facet of my life. I got the loveliest response, part of which I relay here:

And you are right, I have no awareness of what impact I have made in my desire to be of service. And indeed, there are many that have blessed my <u>own</u> life that do not know how much they have helped me. We each stand on the shoulders of those that have gone before. Not one of us is successful except for others.

I realized just then as I read this, that with all of my books, I have been agreeing to be the shoulders for my readers to stand on and launch from, just as many shoulders have preceded me. That I too am a part of this chain that links from the present to centuries past, makes information transformative. That long before there was an internet, people gathered together to share stories and insights to better navigate this wild and wonderous human life. I am so honored to be a part of a sacred tradition of asking the Big Questions. Who am I? What am I here for? How do I do what I came to do? How do I become my True Essence? How do I experience happiness? It's in asking the Big Questions that we open up the flow for the Universe to answer. And often the Big Questions come out of the suffering of feeling different. Out of this suffering, out of seeking relief, the Big Answers come, not just for us but for everyone we are brave enough to share with. This is the M2T journey.

I wanted to introduce you to two real, still-living people you have likely not heard of. (If you are fortunate enough to have come across them, give thanks!) And they have each positively affected thousands if not hundreds of thousands of lives. Every student, every client whose lives they touched, whose energy they affected, went back into their own lives changed, and that made an invisible difference in every person that student encountered. Imagine the proverbial pebble dropped in still water and the ripple effect that unfolds as a result. Undulating rings and waves expanding out in all directions. They accomplished this not with a reality show or Fortune 500 company. Not with a huge social media following or millions of dollars behind them. It all came from the simple and humble act of teaching and serving others with what they found beneficial. Every act an act of love. Every act an act of service to the greater good.

You can become just such a person, if you're not right now. You already have the divine blueprint and plans within you. That's *why* you're different. You came to lead, not follow.

Which brings me to a very important point. For much of this book, I've asked you to see if you can find yourself in the stories and information I've shared. I've encouraged you to explore with the M2T Journal Moments your history and experiences. Most important, I've encouraged you to express your feelings and show up for yourself. Now I'm asking for something more.

There are people out there who need you. Yes, you! There is service and love and encouragement that only you can provide in the way you can provide it. There are creative acts waiting to be born. Not just for you but for the others whose lives you're here to touch. Your rising isn't just for you. There are times when knowing this keeps me going, forging ahead into uncharted territories. There are times it's much easier for me to rise for others than for myself.

See yourself as that pebble. It's when we are in service that we most easily forget our own isolating insecurities. It's then that we can commit our greatest feats. We *must* move out of our wounds and fears to take a stand for the people we are here for.

May you take what you have learned in this book to further your mission, to realize more of your true self, to shed the barriers and blocks, to embrace a path of radical self-love. May you boldly step forward to become the Trailblazer you came here to be. May you lose the hyper self-focus of the small self by falling in love with service to others. May you strut this earth as you truly are, without apology or explanation. May your hidden gifts emerge from within just as you are ready to receive and use them. May you find freedom in all forms of expression. May your true community of people immediately recognize and embrace you with, "Where have you been all my life?" May you always know how much you *matter*. That your very existence means something extremely good is operating in this world.

May you always know you are loved.

Resources

Visit www.yourdifferenceisyourstrength.com for many absolutely free resources, including downloadable PDFs, memes, audios, and videos to support your M2T journey.

MY BOOKS

For Your Humanness

I'm going to start with books by yours truly because I genuinely believe they fit together perfectly with what is in your hands.

Energy Healing is the perfect introduction to energy psychology and emotional processing. See how quickly you can change how you feel and what you believe using your hands and body.

For Your Spirit

Manifesting: I distilled my vast metaphysical principles and practices into one powerful volume demonstrating how to create your best life ever. It comes with many free resources like PDFs, memes, and meditation-visualization audios. See www.manifestingbook.com.

OTHER BOOKS

The Misfit Economy by Alexa Clay and Kyra Maya Phillips

The Myth of Normal by Gabor Mate

The Body Keeps the Score by Bessel van der Kolk

The Artist's Way by Julia Cameron

Radical Forgiveness by Colin Tipping

Acknowledgments

Forever grateful to Great Spirit for this vocation I've been given, the people it has enabled me to serve, and how enormously happy it makes me. In times of doubt and struggle, a part of every creative process, I always know where to go for respite and inspiration. It makes all the difference in the world. I get to tell people they're loved and that's because I am too. Thank you.

Joel Fotinos, I joke that the Universe said, "Let's do something that will really blow her mind! We'll tap Joel on the shoulder and give him an idea to give her a book and ensure her life will be forever changed." I somehow ended up with an editor whose brilliance, talent, and intuition mixed with unending kindness has uplifted and supported me, especially with this one, in ways that continue to astound me. Thank you so, so much, for everything. And for Emily Anderson, who came onto the scene with high professionalism and a much-needed attention to detail while providing a rock-solid foundation for getting it all done. You've been such a gift! Thank you.

Ulana Zahajkewycz, my dear, sweet and enormously talented friend, thank you for these incredible illustrations that make my work pop. Who knew when we created a Riot-Grrl-esque zine in the nineties that we'd be working together again in print all these years later. I have a habit now of calling on my best friends to provide book art, at a moment's notice, and only during major life transitions. That you came through so perfectly wasn't a surprise. Grateful for all our years together and your major contribution here.

For Veronique Ramsey, for always loving me and knowing I can do what I doubt I can. You handle my frustrations and insecurities with so much grace and patience. Thank you!

For Chris Salek, who texted and called at exactly the right moment throughout this writing process. Your intuition is unparalleled! I hope you like that I shared about our first meeting. I always have said, if I was ever arrested, you'd be there to bail me out and shout my innocence from the rooftops. You've had my back since day one. Florida did something right.

For Stephanie Farren, for coming back into my life, cheering me on 100 percent, introducing me to the most extraordinary people, and making every trip back to my second home one filled with laughter, joy and love. You're the best!

For my family, who understands when I miss reunions and vanish to spend weeks hunched over a laptop, thank you for loving and supporting me.

For the many friends who offered not only encouragement, but practical strategies in the writing of this book. Mary Kay Carney and Donniee Barnes, thank you for the texts, hugs, and important conversations around the dining room table. You are a blessing.

For my energy and healing friends and colleagues who offer kindness, connection, encouragement, and celebration, including but not limited to Agnes Brophy, Alicia North, Bonnie Durkin, Cat Stone, Cynthia Jenkins, Jennifer Elizabeth Moore, and Jondi Whitis, you all make me thrilled to be in this incredible company.

And speaking of Jennifer Elizabeth Moore, my sister in empathy, there aren't enough words in the world to thank you for your unwavering support, incredible ideas, remarkable resourcefulness, and endless kindnesses you've bestowed upon me as we've embarked on our most unique author journeys. When I was stuck, your interviewing me about this book jump-started the most important period of writing. And your generosity with lending me so many of your platforms to share my work is so cherished. Plus, you're a safe space for some big, ugly cries! Thank you.

For my spiritual community, Rockland Centers for Spiritual Living, and all my sisters in Spirit there. Your many prayers and gentle guidance saw me through. I am beyond honored to be among you. With huge love to Reverend Melissa Moorer-Nobles, Jan Sheehan, Michelle Ruiz, Janet Squilanti, Cheryl Reuben, Susi Rachouh, and Amy Horan.

About the Author

Lee Seidenberg

KRIS FERRARO is an author, an international energy coach, a spiritual teacher, and a sought-after speaker. After leaving a lengthy career as a social service counselor to guide others in the energy and metaphysical practices she used to heal herself, Kris transitioned to empowering others through the profound promise that everyone can move from surviving to thriving. She frequently speaks to diverse groups on how purpose, love, faith, and balanced energy are the ancient antidotes to modern stress caused by our climate of constant uncertainty. For more than fifteen years, she's used cutting-edge strategies with thousands of one-on-one clients in her coaching practice, assisting them in healing from stubborn anxiety, grief, creative blocks, and disempowerment. A former punk rock radio DJ and performance artist, she discovered it was in healing her severe social anxiety that she was finally able to uncover her purpose and truly shine, without panic. In addition to writing and creating curricula on transformation and producing a content-rich newsletter with original photography, she writes and performs spoken-word poetry and is a ceramic sculptor. When not traveling, she lives in Montclair, New Jersey, with her cats, Ling and The Baby Cheetah. Her first book, *Energy Healing: Simple & Effective Practices to Become Your Own Healer*, was a number-one bestseller on Amazon. Her second, *Manifesting: The Practical, Simple Guide to Creating the Life You Want*, distills ten years of her best metaphysical teachings. *Your Difference Is Your Strength* is her love letter to all Misfits, inspiring them to rise up and become the Trailblazers they were destined to be.

You can learn more about Kris's programs, courses, books, and services at:

WWW.KRISFERRARO.COM

WWW.YOURDIFFERENCEISYOURSTRENGTH.COM

WWW.MANIFESTINGBOOK.COM

Find Kris on social media at:

FACEBOOK: WWW.FACEBOOK.COM/KRIS.FERRARO

FACEBOOK COMMUNITY: WWW.FACEBOOK.COM/BEFREETOFLOURISH/

INSTAGRAM: WWW.INSTAGRAM.COM/KRISEFT/

Megan McNally